WALL STREET
STORIES
BY
EDWIN LEFÈVRE

D1736592

NEW YORK
McCLURE, PHILLIPS & CO.
1901

First Impression October, 1901
Second Impression November, 1901
Third Impression November, 1901

Printing Statement:

Due to the very old age and scarcity of this book,
many of the pages may be hard to read due to the
blurring of the original text, possible missing pages,
missing text, dark backgrounds and other issues
beyond our control.

Because this is such an important and rare work, we
believe it is best to reproduce this book regardless of
its original condition.

Thank you for your understanding.

TO

Samuel Hughes Watts

CONTENTS

THE WOMAN AND HER BONDS

THE WOMAN AND HER BONDS

IT seemed to Fullerton F. Colwell, of the famous Stock-Exchange house of Wilson & Graves, that he had done his full duty by his friend Harry Hunt. He was a director in a half score of companies — financial *débutantes* which his firm had "brought out" and over whose stock-market destinies he presided. His partners left a great deal to him, and even the clerks in the office ungrudgingly acknowledged that Mr. Colwell was "the hardest worked man in the place, barring none" — an admission that means much to those who know it is always the downtrodden clerks who do all the work and their employers who take all the profit and credit. Possibly the important young men who did all the work in Wilson & Graves' office bore witness to Mr. Colwell's industry so cheerfully, because Mr. Colwell was ever inquiring, very courteously, and, above all, sympathetically, into the amount of work each man had to perform, and suggesting, the next moment, that the laborious amount in question was indisputably excessive. Also, it was he who raised salaries ; wherefore he was the most charming as well as the busiest man

3

there.   Of his partners, John G. Wilson was a
consumptive, forever going from one health resort
to another, devoting his millions to the purchase
of railroad tickets in the hope of out-racing Death.
George B. Graves was a dyspeptic, nervous, irritable, and, to boot, penurious ; a man whose chief
recommendation at the time Wilson formed the
firm had been his cheerful willingness to do all the
dirty work.   Frederick R. Denton was busy in the
" Board Room "— the Stock Exchange — all day,
executing orders, keeping watch over the market
behavior of the stocks with which the firm was
identified, and from time to time hearing things
not meant for his ears, being the truth regarding
Wilson & Graves.   But Fullerton F. Colwell had
to do everything — in the stock market and in the
office.   He conducted the manipulation of the
Wilson & Graves stocks, took charge of the un-
nefarious part of the numerous pools formed by
the firm's customers — Mr. Graves attending to the
other details — and had a hand in the actual management of various corporations.   Also, he con-
ferred with a dozen people daily — chiefly " big
people," in Wall Street parlance — who were about
to " put through " stock-market " deals."   He
had devoted his time, which was worth thousands,
and his brain, which was worth millions, to disen-

tangling his careless friend's affairs, and when it
was all over and every claim adjusted, and he had
refused the executor's fees to which he was entitled, it was found that poor Harry Hunt's estate
not only was free from debt, but consisted of
$38,000 in cash, deposited in the Trolleyman's
Trust Company, subject to Mrs. Hunt's order, and
drawing interest at the rate of $2\frac{1}{2}$ per cent per
annum.   He had done his work wonderfully well,
and, in addition to the cash, the widow owned an
unencumbered house Harry had given her in his
lifetime.

Not long after the settlement of the estate Mrs.
Hunt called at his office.   It was a very busy day.
The bears were misbehaving — and misbehaving
mighty successfully.   Alabama Coal & Iron — the
firm's great specialty — was under heavy fire from
"Sam" Sharpe's Long Tom as well as from the
room-traders' Maxims.   All that Colwell could
do was to instruct Denton, who was on the ground,
to "support" *Ala. C. & I.* sufficiently to discour-
age the enemy, and not enough to acquire the
company's entire capital stock.   He was himself
at that moment practising that peculiar form of
financial dissimulation which amounts to singing
blithely at the top of your voice when your be-
loved sackful of gold has been ripped by bear-

paws and the coins are pouring out through the
rent. Every quotation was of importance ; a half
inch of tape might contain an epic of disaster. It
was not wise to fail to read every printed character.

"Good morning, Mr. Colwell."

He ceased to pass the tape through his fingers,
and turned quickly, almost apprehensively, for a
woman's voice was not heard with pleasure at an
hour of the day when distractions were undesir-
able.

"Ah, good morning, Mrs. Hunt," he said, very
politely. "I am very glad indeed to see you.
And how do you do ? " He shook hands, and led
her, a bit ceremoniously, to a huge armchair.
His manners endeared him even to the big Wall
Street operators, who were chiefly interested in the
terse speech of the ticker.

"Of course, you are very well, Mrs. Hunt.
Don't tell me you are not."

"Ye-es," hesitatingly. "As well as I can hope
to be since — since —— "

"Time alone, dear Mrs. Hunt, can help us.
You must be very brave. It is what he would
have liked."

"Yes, I know," she sighed. "I suppose I
must."

There was a silence. He stood by, deferentially sympathetic.

"*Ticky-ticky-ticky-tick*," said the ticker.

What did it mean, in figures? Reduced to dollars and cents, what did the last three brassy taps say? Perhaps the bears were storming the Alabama Coal & Iron intrenchments of "scaled buying orders"; perhaps Colwell's trusted lieutenant, Fred Denton, had repulsed the enemy. Who was winning? A spasm, as of pain, passed over Mr. Fullerton F. Colwell's grave face. But the next moment he said to her, slightly conscience-strickenly, as if he reproached himself for thinking of the stock market in her presence: "You must not permit yourself to brood, Mrs. Hunt. You know what I thought of Harry, and I need not tell you how glad I shall be to do what I may, for his sake, Mrs. Hunt, and for your own."

"*Ticky-ticky-ticky-tick!*" repeated the ticker.

To avoid listening to the voluble little machine, he went on: "Believe me, Mrs. Hunt, I shall be only too glad to serve you."

"You are so kind, Mr. Colwell," murmured the widow; and after a pause: "I came to see you about that money."

"Yes?"

"They tell me in the trust company that if I

leave the money there without touching it I'll make $79 a month."

"Let me see; yes; that is about what you may expect."

"Well, Mr. Colwell, I can't live on that. Willie's school costs me $50, and then there's Edith's clothes," she went on, with an air which implied that as for herself she wouldn't care at all. "You see, he was so indulgent, and they are used to so much. Of course, it's a blessing we have the house; but taxes take up so much; and — isn't there some way of investing the money so it could bring more?"

"I might buy some bonds for you. But for your principal to be absolutely safe at all times, you will have to invest in very high-grade securities, which will return to you about $3\frac{1}{2}$ per cent. That would mean, let's see, $110 a month."

"And Harry spent $10,000 a year," she murmured, complainingly.

"Harry was always — er — rather extravagant."

"Well, I'm glad he enjoyed himself while he lived," she said, quickly. Then, after a pause: "And, Mr. Colwell, if I should get tired of the bonds, could I always get my money back?"

"You could always find a ready market for

them. You might sell them for a little more or for a little less than you paid."

" I shouldn't like to sell them," she said, with a business air, "for less than I paid. What would be the sense?"

" You are right, Mrs. Hunt," he said, encouragingly. "It wouldn't be very profitable, would it?"

" *Ticky-ticky-ticky-ticky-ticky-ticky-tick!* " said the ticker. It was whirring away at a furious rate. Its story is always interesting when it is busy. And Colwell had not looked at the tape in fully five minutes!

" Couldn't you buy something for me, Mr. Colwell, that when I came to sell it I could get more than it cost me?"

" No man can guarantee that, Mrs. Hunt."

" I shouldn't like to lose the little I have," she said, hastily.

" Oh, there is no danger of that. If you will give me a check for $35,000, leaving $3,000 with the trust company for emergencies, I shall buy some bonds which I feel reasonably certain will advance in price within a few months."

" *Ticky-ticky-ticky-tick,*" interrupted the ticker. In some inexplicable way it seemed to him that the brassy sound had an ominous ring, so he added: "But you will have to let me know promptly, Mrs. Hunt. The stock market, you see, is not a polite institution. It waits for none, not even for your sex."

"Gracious me, must I take the money out of the bank to-day and bring it to you?"

"A check will do." He began to drum on the desk nervously with his fingers, but ceased abruptly as he became aware of it.

"Very well, I'll send it to you to-day. I know you're very busy, so I won't keep you any longer. And you'll buy good, cheap bonds for me?"

"Yes, Mrs. Hunt."

"There's no danger of losing, is there, Mr. Colwell?"

"None whatever. I have bought some for Mrs. Colwell, and I would not run the slightest risk. You need have no fear about them."

"It's exceedingly kind of you, Mr. Colwell. I am more grateful than I can say. I — I —— "

"The way to please me is not to mention it, Mrs. Hunt. I am going to try to make some money for you, so that you can at least double the income from the trust company."

"Thanks, ever so much. Of course, I know you are thoroughly familiar with such things. But I've heard so much about the money everybody loses in Wall Street that I was half afraid."

"Not when you buy good bonds, Mrs. Hunt."

"Good morning, Mr. Colwell."

"Good morning, Mrs. Hunt. Remember, whenever I may be of service you are to let me know immediately."

"Oh, thank you, so much, Mr. Colwell. Good morning."

"Good morning, Mrs. Hunt."

Mrs. Hunt sent him a check for $35,000, and Colwell bought 100 five-per cent gold bonds of the Manhattan Electric Light, Heat & Power Company, paying 96 for them.

"These bonds," he wrote to her, "will surely advance in price, and when they touch a good figure I shall sell a part, and keep the balance for you as an investment. The operation is partly speculative, but I assure you the money is safe. You will have an opportunity to increase your original capital and your entire funds will then be invested in these same bonds — Manhattan Electric 5s — as many as the money will buy. I hope within six months to secure for you an income of twice as much as you have been receiving from the trust company."

The next morning she called at his office.

"Good morning, Mrs. Hunt.   I trust you are well."

"Good morning, Mr. Colwell.   I know I am an awful bother to you, but —— "

" You are greatly mistaken, Mrs. Hunt."

" You are very kind.   You see, I don't exactly understand about those bonds.   I thought you could tell me.   I'm so stupid," archly.

" I won't have you prevaricate about yourself, Mrs. Hunt.   Now, you gave me $35,000, didn't you ? "

" Yes."   Her tone indicated that she granted that much and nothing more.

" Well, I opened an account for you with our firm.   You were credited with the amount.   I then gave an order to buy one hundred bonds of $1,000 each.   We paid 96 for them."

" I don't follow you quite, Mr. Colwell.   I told you " — another arch smile — " I was so stupid ! "

" It means that for each $1,000-bond $960 was paid.   It brought the total up to $96,000."

" But I only had $35,000 to begin with.   You don't mean I've made that much, do you ? "

" Not yet, Mrs. Hunt.   You put in $35,000 ; that was your margin, you know ; and we put in the other $61,000 and kept the bonds as security. We owe you $35,000, and you owe us $61,000, and —— "

" But — I know you'll laugh at me, Mr. Colwell — but I really can't help thinking it's something like the poor people you read about, who mortgage their houses, and they go on, and the first thing you know some real-estate agent owns the house and you have nothing. I have a friend, Mrs. Stilwell, who lost hers that way," she finished, corroboratively.

"This is not a similar case, exactly. The reason why you use a margin is that you can do much more with the money that way than if you bought outright. It protects your broker against a depreciation in the security purchased, which is all he wants. In this case you theoretically owe us $61,000, but the bonds are in your name, and they are worth $96,000, so that if you want to pay us back, all you have to do is to order us to sell the bonds, return the money we have advanced, and keep the balance of your margin ; that is, of your original sum."

"I don't understand why I should owe the firm. I shouldn't mind so much owing you, because I know you'd never take advantage of my ignorance of business matters. But I've never met Mr. Wilson nor Mr. Graves. I don't even know how they look."

"But you know me," said Mr. Colwell, with patient courtesy.

"Oh, it isn't that I'm afraid of being cheated, Mr. Colwell," she said hastily and reassuringly; "but I don't wish to be under obligations to any one, particularly utter strangers; though, of course, if you say it is all right, I am satisfied."

"My dear Mrs. Hunt, don't worry about this matter. We bought these bonds at 96. If the price should advance to 110, as I think it will, then you can sell three fifths for $66,000, pay us back $61,000, and keep $5,000 for emergencies in savings banks drawing 4 per cent interest, and have in addition 40 bonds which will pay you $2,000 a year."

"That would be lovely. And the bonds are now 96?"

"Yes; you will always find the price in the financial page of the newspapers, where it says BONDS. Look for *Man. Elec. 5s*," and he showed her.

"Oh, thanks, ever so much. Of course, I am a great bother, I know ——"

"You are nothing of the kind, Mrs. Hunt. I'm only too glad to be of the slightest use to you."

Mr. Colwell, busy with several important deals, did not follow closely the fluctuations in the price of Manhattan Electric Light, Heat &

Power Company 5s. The fact that there had been any change at all was made clear to him by Mrs. Hunt. She called a few days after her first visit, with perturbation written large on her face. Also, she wore the semi-resolute look of a person who expects to hear unacceptable excuses.

"Good morning, Mr. Colwell."

"How do you do, Mrs. Hunt? Well, I hope."

"Oh, I am well enough. I wish I could say as much for my financial matters." She had acquired the phrase from the financial reports which she had taken to reading religiously every day.

"Why, how is that?"

"They are 95 now," she said, a trifle accusingly.

"Who are *they*, pray, Mrs. Hunt?" in surprise.

"The bonds. I saw it in last night's paper."

Mr. Colwell smiled. Mrs. Hunt almost became indignant at his levity.

"Don't let that worry you, Mrs. Hunt. The bonds are all right. The market is a trifle dull; that's all."

"A friend," she said, very slowly, "who knows all about Wall Street, told me last night that it made a difference of $1,000 to me."

"So it does, in a way; that is, if you tried to sell your bonds.   But as you are not going to do so until they show you a handsome profit, you need not worry.   Don't be concerned about the matter, I beg of you.   When the time comes for you to sell the bonds I'll let you know.   Never mind if the price goes off a point or two.   You are amply protected.   Even if there should be a panic I'll see that you are not sold out, no matter how low the price goes.   You are not to worry about it; in fact, you are not to think about it at all."

"Oh, thanks, ever so much, Mr. Colwell.   I didn't sleep a wink last night.   But I knew —— "

A clerk came in with some stock certificates and stopped short.   He wanted Mr. Colwell's signature in a hurry, and at the same time dared not interrupt.   Mrs. Hunt thereupon rose and said : " Well, I won't take up any more of your time.   Good morning, Mr. Colwell.   Thanks ever so much."

"Don't mention it, Mrs. Hunt.   Good morning.   You are going to do very well with those bonds if you only have patience."

"Oh, I'll be patient now that I know all about it; yes, indeed.   And I hope your prophecy will be fulfilled.   Good morning, Mr. Colwell."

Little by little the bonds continued to decline.
The syndicate in charge was not ready to move
them. But Mrs. Hunt's unnamed friend — her
Cousin Emily's husband — who was employed in
an up-town bank, did not know all the particulars
of that deal. He knew the Street in the ab-
stract, and had accordingly implanted the seed of
insomnia in her quaking soul. Then, as he saw
values decline, he did his best to make the seed
grow, fertilizing a naturally rich soil with ominous hints and head-shakings and with phrases
that made her firmly believe he was gradually and
considerately preparing her for the worst. On the
third day of her agony Mrs. Hunt walked into
Colwell's office. Her face was pale and she looked
distressed. Mr. Colwell sighed involuntarily — a
scarcely perceptible and not very impolite sigh —
and said : "Good morning, Mrs. Hunt."

She nodded gravely and, with a little gasp, said,
tremulously : "The bonds !"

"Yes ? What about them ?"

She gasped again, and said : "The p-p-pa-
pers !"

"What do you mean, Mrs. Hunt ?"

She dropped into a chair nervelessly, as if ex-
hausted. After a pause she said : "It's in all the
papers. I thought the *Herald* might be mistaken,

so I bought the *Tribune* and the *Times* and the *Sun*. But no. It was the same in all. It was," she added, tragically, " 93 ! "

" Yes ? " he said, smilingly.

The smile did not reassure her ; it irritated her and aroused her suspicions. By him, of all men, should her insomnia be deemed no laughing matter.

" Doesn't that mean a loss of $3,000 ? " she asked. There was a deny-it-if-you-dare inflection in her voice of which she was not conscious. Her cousin's husband had been a careful gardener.

" No, because you are not going to sell your bonds at 93, but at 110, or thereabouts."

" But if I did want to sell the bonds now, wouldn't I lose $3,000 ? " she queried, challengingly. Then she hastened to answer herself: " Of course I would, Mr. Colwell. Even I can tell that."

" You certainly would, Mrs. Hunt ; but —— "

" I knew I was right," with irrepressible triumph.

" But you are not going to sell the bonds."

" Of course, I don't want to, because I can't afford to lose any money, much less $3,000. But I don't see how I can help losing it. I was warned from the first," she said, as if that made it worse. "I certainly had no business to risk my all." She had waived the right to blame some one else, and there was something consciously just and judicial about her attitude that was eloquent. Mr. Colwell was moved by it.

"You can have your money back, Mrs. Hunt, if you wish it," he told her, quite unprofessionally. "You seem to worry about it so much."

"Oh, I am not worrying, exactly ; only, I do wish I hadn't bought — I mean, the money was so safe in the Trolleyman's Trust Company, that I can't help thinking I might just as well have let it stay where it was, even if it didn't bring me in so much. But, of course, if you want me to leave it here," she said, very slowly to give him every opportunity to contradict her, "of course, I'll do just as you say."

"My dear Mrs. Hunt," Colwell said, very politely, "my only desire is to please you and to help you. When you buy bonds you must be prepared to be patient. It may take months before you will be able to sell yours at a profit, and I don't know how low the price will go in the meantime. Nobody can tell you that, because nobody knows. But it need make no difference to you whether the bonds go to 90, or even to 85, which is unlikely."

"Why, how can you say so, Mr. Colwell? If the bonds go to 90, I'll lose $6,000 — my friend said it was one thousand for every number down. And at 85 that would be" — counting on her fingers — "eleven numbers, that is, *eleven — thousand — dollars!*" And she gazed at him, awe-strickenly, reproachfully. "How *can* you say it would make no difference, Mr. Colwell?"

Mr. Colwell fiercely hated the unnamed "friend," who had told her so little and yet so much. But he said to her, mildly: "I thought that I had explained all that to you. It might hurt a weak speculator if the bonds declined ten points, though such a decline is utterly improbable. But it won't affect you in the slightest, since, having an ample margin, you would not be forced to sell. You would simply hold on until the price rose again. Let me illustrate. Supposing your house cost $10,000, and——"

"Harry paid $32,000," she said, correctingly. On second thought she smiled, in order to let him see that she knew her interpolation was irrelevant. But he might as well know the actual cost.

"Very well," he said, good-humoredly, "we'll say $32,000, which was also the price of every other house in that block. And suppose that,

owing to some accident, or for any reason whatever, nobody could be found to pay more than
$25,000 for one of the houses, and three or four
of your neighbors sold theirs at that price.   But
you wouldn't, because you knew that in the fall,
when everybody came back to town, you would
find plenty of people who'd give you $50,000 for
your house; you wouldn't sell it for $25,000, and
you wouldn't worry.   Would you, now?" he finished, cheerfully.

"No," she said slowly.   "I wouldn't worry.
But," hesitatingly, for, after all, she felt the awk-
wardness of her position, "I wish I had the money
instead of the bonds."   And she added, self-defen-
sively : "I haven't slept a wink for three nights
thinking about this."

The thought of his coming emancipation cheered
Mr. Colwell immensely.   "Your wish shall be
gratified, Mrs. Hunt.   Why didn't you ask me
before, if you felt that way?" he said, in mild re-
proach.   And he summoned a clerk.

"Make out a check for $35,000 payable to
Mrs. Rose Hunt, and transfer the 100 Manhattan
Electric Light 5s to my personal account."

He gave her the check and told her : "Here is
the money.   I am very sorry that I unwittingly
caused you some anxiety.   But all's well that

ends well.   Any time that I can be of service to
you — Not at all.   Don't thank me, please ; no.
Good morning."

But he did not tell her that by taking over her
account he paid $96,000 for bonds he could have
bought in the open market for $93,000.   He was
the politest man in Wall Street ; and, after all,
he had known Hunt for many years.

A week later Manhattan Electric 5-per cent
bonds sold at 96 again.   Mrs. Hunt called on
him.   It was noon, and she evidently had spent
the morning mustering up courage for the visit.
They greeted one another, she embarrassed and
he courteous and kindly as usual.

"Mr. Colwell, you still have those bonds, haven't
you ? "

" Why, yes."

" I — I think I'd like to take them back."

" Certainly, Mrs. Hunt.   I'll find out how much
they are selling for."   He summoned a clerk to
get a quotation on Manhattan Electric 5s.   The
clerk telephoned to one of their bond-specialists,
and learned that the bonds could be bought at
96½.   He reported to Mr. Colwell, and Mr. Colwell told Mrs. Hunt, adding : " So you see they
are practically where they were when you bought
them before."

She hesitated. "I—I—didn't you buy them from me at 93? I'd like to buy them back at the same price I sold them to you."

"No, Mrs. Hunt," he said; "I bought them from you at 96."

"But the price was 93." And she added, corroboratively: "Don't you remember it was in all the papers?"

"Yes, but I gave you back exactly the same amount that I received from you, and I had the bonds transferred to my account. They stand on our books as having cost me 96."

"But couldn't you let me have them at 93?" she persisted.

"I'm very sorry, Mrs. Hunt, but I don't see how I could. If you buy them in the open market now, you will be in exactly the same position as before you sold them, and you will make 'a great deal of money, because they are going up now. Let me buy them for you at 96½."

"At 93, you mean," with a tentative smile.

"At whatever price they may be selling for," he corrected, patiently.

"Why did you let me sell them, Mr. Colwell?" she asked, plaintively.

"But, my dear madam, if you buy them now,

you will be no worse off than if you had kept the original lot."

"Well, I don't see why it is that I have to pay 96½ now for the very same bonds I sold last Tuesday at 93. If it was some other bonds," she added, "I wouldn't mind so much."

"My dear Mrs. Hunt, it makes no difference which bonds you hold. They have all risen in price, yours and mine and everybody's; your lot was the same as any other lot. You see that, don't you?"

"Ye–es; but —— "

"Well, then, you are exactly where you were before you bought any. You've lost nothing, because you received your money back intact."

"I'm willing to buy them," she said resolutely, "at 93."

"Mrs. Hunt, I wish I could buy them for you at that price. But there are none for sale cheaper than 96½."

"Oh, why did I let you sell my bonds!" she said, disconsolately.

"Well, you worried so much because they had declined that —— "

"Yes, but I didn't know anything about business matters. You know I didn't, Mr. Colwell," she finished, accusingly.

He smiled in his good-natured way. "Shall I buy the bonds for you?" he asked. He knew the plans of the syndicate in charge, and being sure the bonds would advance, he thought she might as well share in the profits. At heart he felt sorry for her.

She smiled back. "Yes," she told him, "at 93." It did not seem right to her, notwithstanding his explanations, that she should pay $96\frac{1}{2}$ for them, when the price a few days ago was 93.

"But how can I, if they are $96\frac{1}{2}$?"

"Mr. Colwell, it is 93 or nothing." She was almost pale at her own boldness. It really seemed to her as if the price had only been waiting for her to sell out in order to advance. And though she wanted the bonds, she did not feel like yielding.

"Then I very much fear it will have to be nothing."

"Er—good morning, Mr. Colwell," on the verge of tears.

"Good morning, Mrs. Hunt." And before he knew it, forgetting all that had gone before, he added: "Should you change your mind, I should be glad to ——"

"I know I wouldn't pay more than 93 if I lived to be a thousand years." She looked expectantly at him, to see if he had repented, and she smiled

— the smile that is a woman's last resort, that
says, almost articulately: "I know you will, of
course, do as I ask. My question is only a for-
mality. I know your nobility, and I fear not."
But he only bowed her out, very politely.

On the Stock Exchange the price of *Man. Elec.
L. H. & P. Co. 5s* rose steadily. Mrs. Hunt, too
indignant to feel lachrymose, discussed the subject
with her Cousin Emily and her husband. Emily
was very much interested. Between her and Mrs.
Hunt they forced the poor man to make strange
admissions, and, deliberately ignoring his feeble
protests, they worked themselves up to the point
of believing that, while it would be merely generous of Mr. Colwell to let his friend's widow have
the bonds at 93, it would be only his obvious duty
to let her have them at $96\frac{1}{2}$. The moment they
reached this decision Mrs. Hunt knew how to act.
And the more she thought the more indignant she
became. The next morning she called on her late
husband's executor and friend.

Her face wore the look often seen on those
ardent souls who think their sacred and inaliena-
ble rights have been trampled upon by the tyrant
Man, but who at the same time feel certain the
hour of retribution is near.

"Good morning, Mr. Colwell. I came to find

out exactly what you propose to do about my
bonds." Her voice conveyed the impression that
she expected violent opposition, perhaps even bad
language, from him.

"Good morning, Mrs. Hunt. Why, what do
you mean?"

His affected ignorance deepened the lines on
her face. Instead of bluster he was using *finesse!*

"I think you ought to know, Mr. Colwell," she
said, meaningly.

"Well, I really don't. I remember you wouldn't
heed my advice when I told you not to sell out,
and again when I advised you to buy them
back."

"Yes, at $96\frac{1}{2}$," she burst out, indignantly.

"Well, if you had, you would to-day have a
profit of over $7,000."

"And whose fault is it that I haven't?" She
paused for a reply. Receiving none, she went on:
"But never mind; I have decided to accept your
offer," very bitterly, as if a poor widow could not
afford to be a chooser; "I'll take those bonds at
$96\frac{1}{2}$." And she added, under her breath: "Al-
though it really ought to be 93."

"But, Mrs. Hunt," said Colwell, in measureless
astonishment, "you can't do that, you know. You
wouldn't buy them when I wanted you to, and I

can't buy them for you now at 96½.   Really, you
ought to see that."

Cousin Emily and she had gone over a dozen
imaginary interviews with Mr. Colwell — of varying degrees of storminess — the night before, and
they had, in an idle moment, and not because they
really expected it, represented Mr. Colwell as taking
that identical stand.   Mrs. Hunt was, accordingly,
prepared to show both that she knew her moral
and technical rights, and that she was ready to
resist any attempt to ignore them.   So she said,
in a voice so ferociously calm that it should have
warned any guilty man : "Mr. Colwell, will you
answer me one question?"

"A thousand, Mrs. Hunt, with pleasure."

"No; only one.   Have you kept the bonds
that I bought, or have you not?"

"What difference does that make, Mrs. Hunt?"
He evaded the answer!

"Yes or no, please.   Have you, or have you
not, those same identical bonds?"

"Yes; I have.   But —— "

"And to whom do those bonds belong, by
rights?"   She was still pale, but resolute.

" To me, certainly."

" To *you*, Mr. Colwell?"   She smiled.   And in
her smile were a thousand feelings; but not mirth.

"Yes, Mrs. Hunt, to me."

"And do you propose to keep them?"

"I certainly do."

"Not even if I pay 96½ will you give them to me?"

"Mrs. Hunt," Colwell said with warmth "when I took those bonds off your hands at 93 it represented a loss on paper of $3,000 ——"

She smiled in pity — pity for his judgment in thinking her so hopelessly stupid.

"And when you wanted me to sell them back to you at 93 after they had risen to 96½, if I had done as you wished, it would have meant an actual loss of $3,000 to me."

Again she smiled — the same smile, only the pity was now mingled with rising indignation.

"For Harry's sake I was willing to pocket the first loss, in order that you might not worry. But I didn't see why I should make you a present of $3,000," he said, very quietly.

"I never asked you to do it," she retorted, hotly.

"If you had lost any money through my fault, it would have been different. But you had your original capital unimpaired. You had nothing to lose, if you bought back the same bonds at practically the same price. Now you come and ask me to sell you the bonds at 96½ that are selling in the market for 104, as a reward, I suppose, for your refusal to take my advice."

"Mr. Colwell, you take advantage of my position to insult me. And Harry trusted you so much! But let me tell you that I am not going to let you do just as you please. No doubt you would like to have me go home and forget how you've acted toward me. But I am going to consult a lawyer, and see if I am to be treated this way by a *friend* of my husband's. You've made a mistake, Mr. Colwell."

"Yes, madam, I certainly have. And, in order to avoid making any more, you will oblige me greatly by never again calling at this office. By all means consult a lawyer. Good morning, madam," said the politest man in Wall Street.

"We'll see," was all she said; and she left the room.

Colwell paced up and down his office nervously. It was seldom that he allowed himself to lose his temper, and he did not like it. The ticker whirred away excitedly, and in an absent-minded, half-disgusted way he glanced sideways at it.

"*Man. Elec. 5s, 106$\frac{1}{8}$,*" he read on the tape.

THE BREAK IN TURPENTINE

THE BREAK IN TURPENTINE

IN the beginning of the beginning the distillers of turpentine carried competition to the quarrelling point. Then they carried the quarrel to the point of silence, which was most to be feared, for it meant that no time was to be wasted in words. All were losing money; but each hoped that the others were losing more, proportionately, and therefore would go under all the sooner. The survivors thought they could manage to keep on surviving, for on what twelve would starve four could feast.

It is seen periodically in the United States: an industry apparently suffering from suicidal mania. It is incomprehensible, inexplicable, though mediocrities mutter: "Over-production!" and shake their heads complacently, proud of having diagnosed the trouble. Here was the turpentine business, once great and lucrative, now ruin-producing; formerly affording a comfortable livelihood to many thousands and now giving ever-diminishing wages to ever-diminishing numbers.

It was Mr. Alfred Neustadt, a banker in a famous turpentine district, who first called his

brother-in-law's attention to the pitiable sight.
Mr. Jacob Greenbaum's soul thrilled during Neustadt's recital. He perceived golden possibilities
that dazzled him : He decided to form a Turpentine Trust.

First he bought for a song all the bankrupt
stills ; seven of them. Later on, in his scheme of
trust creation, these self-same distilleries would be
turned over to the "octopus," at nice fat figures,
as Greenbaum put it, self-admiringly, to his
brother-in-law. Then he secured options on nine
others, the tired-unto-death plants. In this way
he was able to control "a large productive capacity" at an expenditure positively marvellous — it
was so small. It was also in his brother-in-law's
name. Then the banking house of Greenbaum,
Lazarus & Co. stepped in, interested accomplices,
duped or coerced into selling enough other distillers to assure success, cajoled the more stubborn,
wheedled the more credulous, gave way gracefully
to the shrewder and gathered them all into the
fold. The American Turpentine Company was
formed, with a capital stock of $30,000,000 or
300,000 shares at $100 each. The cash needed,
to pay Mr. Greenbaum, Neustadt and others who
sold their plants for " part cash and part stock,"
was provided by an issue of $25,000,000 of 6 per

cent bonds, underwritten by a syndicate composed
of Greenbaum, Lazarus & Co., I. & S. Wechsler,
Morris Steinfelder's Sons, Reis & Stern, Kohn,
Fischel & Co., Silberman & Lindheim, Rosenthal,
Shaffran & Co. and Zeman Bros.

They were men who never "speculated"; sometimes they "conducted financial operations." They
had shears, not fleeces.

The prospectus of the "Trust" was a master-
piece of persuasiveness and vagueness, of slim statistics and alluring generalities.   In due course of
time the public subscribed for the greater part of
the $25,000,000 of bonds, and both bonds and
stock were "listed" on the New York Stock Exchange — that is, they were placed on the list of
securities which members may buy or sell on the
" floor " of the Exchange.

Tabularly expressed, the syndicate's operations
were as follows :

Authorized stock.............................$30,000,000
     "   bonds 25,000,000
                                                                        ————————
     Total..$55,000,000
Actual worth of property.................. 12,800,000
                                                                        ————————
     Aqua Pura..............................$42,200,000

Paid to owners for 41 distilleries representing
90 per cent of the turpentine production (and 121

per cent of the consumption!) of the United
States :

Cash from bond sales	$8,975,983
Bonds	12,000,000
Stock	18,249,800
Total	$39,225,783
Syndicate's commission, stock	12,988,500
Retained in Co.'s treasury, unissued	2,000,000
Expenses and discounts on bonds, etc	785,717
Total	$55,000,000

These figures were not for publication. They
told the exact truth.

The public knew nothing of the company's
earning capacity, save a few tentative figures from
the prospectus, which was a sort of financial gos-
pel according to Greenbaum, but which did not
create fanatical devotees among investors. The
stock, unlike the Kipling ship, had not found itself. It was not market-proven, not seasoned ; no
one knew how much dependence to put on it ;
wherefore the banks would not take it as collateral
security on loans and wherefore the "speculative
community" (as the newspapers call the stock
gamblers) would not touch it, since in a pinch it
might prove utterly unvendible. It remained for
the syndicate to make a "market" for it, to de-
velop such a condition of affairs that anyone at

any time could, without overmuch difficulty and without causing over-great fluctuations, sell readily American Turpentine Company stock.   The syndicate would have to earn its commission.

All the manufacturers who had received stock in part payment were told most impressively by Mr. Greenbaum not to sell their holdings under any circumstances at any price below $75 a share. Not knowing Mr. Greenbaum, they readily and solemnly promised to obey him.   They even permitted themselves to think, after talking to him, that they would some day receive $80 per share for all their holdings.   This precluded any untimely " unloading" by the only people outside the syndicate that held any Turpentine stock at all.

Mr. Greenbaum took charge of the market conduct of " Turp," as the tape called the stock of the American Turpentine Company.   At first, the price was marked up by means of " matched" orders — preconcerted and therefore not bona fide transactions.   Mr. Greenbaum told one of his brokers to sell 1,000 shares of " Turp " to another of his brokers and shortly afterwards the second broker sold the same 1,000 shares to a third, by pre-arrangement — this being the matching process — with the result that the tape recorded transac-

tions of 2,000 shares. After the "matching"
had gone on for some time, readers of the tape
were supposed to imagine that the stock was legit-
imately active and strong — two facts which in
turn were supposed to whet the buying appetite.
It was against the rule of the Exchange to
"match" orders, but how could convictions be
secured ?

"Turp" began at 25 and as the syndicate had
all the stock in the market, it was easily manipulated upward to 35. Every day, many thousands of
shares, according to the Stock Exchange's official
records, "changed hands" — from Greenbaum's
right to his left and back again — and the price
rose steadily. But something was absent. The
manipulation was not convincing. It did not
make the general public nibble. The only buyers were the "room traders," that is, the professional stock gamblers who were members of the
Exchange and speculated for themselves exclusively ; and those customers of the commission
houses who, because they were bound to speculate
daily or die and because they studied the ticker-
ribbon so assiduously, were known by the generic
name of "tape-worms." These gentry, in and out
of the Exchange, provided the tape in its curious
language foretold a rise, would buy anything —

from capitalized impudence, as in the case of Back
Bay Gas, whose property was actually worth nil
and its capital stock was $100,000,000, up to
Government bonds.

Now, the room traders and the tape-worms
reasoned not illogically that the "Greenbaum
gang" had all the stock and that perforce the
"gang" had to find a market for it; and the only
way to do this was by a nice "bull" or upward
movement. When a stock rises and rises and
rises the newspapers are full of pleasant stories
about it and the lambs read but do not run away;
they buy on the assumption that, as the stock has
already risen ten points it may rise ten more.
This explains why they make so much money in
Wall Street — for the natives.

Greenbaum and his associates were exceptionally shrewd business men, thoroughly familiar with
Wall Street and its methods, cautious yet bold,
far-seeing yet eminently of the day. They were
practical financiers. They marked up the price
of "Turp" ten points; but they could not arouse
public interest in it so that people would buy it.
Indeed, at the end of three weeks, during which
the "Street" had been flooded with impressive
advice, printed and spoken, to buy because the
price was going higher, all they had for their

trouble was more stock — 6,000 shares from Ira
D. Keep, a distiller, who sold out at 38 because
he needed the money; and they also were obliged
to buy back from the "room traders" at 35 and
36 and higher, the same stock the "gang" had
sold at 30 and 31 and 32 and 34. Then the
manipulators had to "support" the stock at the
higher level, that is, they had to keep it from declining, which could be done only by continuous
buying. By doing this the public might imagine
there was considerable merit in a stock which was
in such good demand from intelligent people as
to remain firm, notwithstanding its previous substantial rise. And if somebody wanted "Turp"
why shouldn't the public want it? The public
generally asks itself that question. It is in the
nature of a nibble and rejoices the hearts of the
financial anglers.

Every attempt to sell "Turp" met with failure.
At length it was decided to allow the price to sink
back to an "invitingly low" level. It was done.
But still the invited public refused to buy. Efforts
to encourage a short interest to over-extend itself
unto "squeezable" proportions failed similarly.
The Street was afraid to go "short" of a stock
which was so closely held. The philosophy of
short selling is simple; it really amounts to bet-

ting that values will decline.   A man who "sells
short" sells what he does not possess, but hopes
to buy, later on, at a lower price.   But since he
must deliver what he sells he borrows it from
some one else, giving the lender ample security.
To "cover" or to "buy in" is to purchase stock
previously sold short.   Obviously, it is unwise to
be short of a stock which is held by such a few
that it may be difficult to borrow it.   To
"squeeze" shorts is to advance the price in order
to force "covering."   This is done when the
short interest is large enough to make it worth
while.

In the course of the next few months, after a
series of injudicious fluctuations which gave to
"Turp" a bad name, even as Wall Street names
went, despite glowing accounts of the company's
wonderful business and after distributing less than
35,000 shares, the members of the "Turpentine
Skindicate," as it was popularly called, sorrowfully
acknowledged that, while they had skilfully
organized the trust and had done fairly well with
the bonds, they certainly were not howling suc-
cesses as manipulators.   During the following
eight months they sold more stock.   They spared
not the widow nor the orphan.   They even
"stuck" their intimate friends.   They had sold

for something what had cost them nothing; it was natural to wish to sell more.

Now, manipulators of stocks are born, not made. The art is most difficult, for stocks should be manipulated in such wise that they will not look manipulated. Anybody can buy stocks or can sell them. But not every one can sell stocks and at the same time convey the impression that he is buying them, and that prices therefore must inevitably go much higher. It requires boldness and consummate judgment, knowledge of technical stock-market conditions, infinite ingenuity and mental agility, absolute familiarity with human nature, a careful study of the curious psychological phenomena of gambling and long experience with the Wall Street public and with the wonderful imagination of the American people; to say nothing of knowing thoroughly the various brokers to be employed, their capabilities, limitations and personal temperaments; also, their price.

Adequate manipulative machinery, moreover, can be perfected only with much toil and patience and money. Professional Wall Street will always tell you that "the tape tells the story." The little paper ribbon, therefore, must be made to tell such stories as the manipulator desires should

be told to the public; he must produce certain
effects which should preserve an appearance of
alluring spontaneity and, above all, of legitimacy
and candor; he must be a great artist in mendacity and at the same time have the superb self-
confidence of a grizzly.

Several members of the syndicate had many of
these qualities, but none had them all.   It was
decided to put "Turp" stock in the hands of
Samuel Wimbleton Sharpe, the best manipulator
Wall Street had ever known.   "Jakey" Greenbaum said he would conduct the negotiations
with the great plunger.

Sharpe was a financial free-lance, free-booter
and free-thinker.   He had made his first fortune
in the mining camps of Arizona and finding that
field too narrow had come to New York, where he
could gamble to his heart's content.   He was all
the things that an ideal manipulator should be
and several more.   He had arrived in New York
with a sneer on his lips and a loaded revolver in
his financial hands.   The other "big operators"
looked at him in pained astonishment.   "I carry
my weapons openly," Sharpe told them, "and you
conceal your dirks.   Don't hurt yourselves trying
to look honest.   I never turn my back on such as
you."   Of this encounter was born a hostility

that never grew faint. Sharpe had nothing of
his own to unload on anyone else, no property to
overcapitalize and sell to an undiscriminating
public by means of artistic lies and his enemies
often did. So they called him a gambler, very
bitterly, and he called them philanthropists, very
cheerfully. If he thought a stock was unduly
high he sold it confidently, aggressively, stupen-
dously. If he thought a stock was too low he
bought it boldly, ready to take all the offerings
and bid for more. And once on the march, he
might be temporarily checked, be forced by the
enemy to halt for a day or a week or a month;
but inevitably he arrived. And such an arrival!

And as a manipulator of stock-values he had no
equal. On the bull side he rushed a stock upward so steadily, so boldly and brilliantly, but,
above all, so persuasively, that lesser gamblers almost fought to be allowed to take it off his hands
at incredibly high prices. And when in the conduct of one of his masterly bear campaigns he saw
fit to "hammer" the market, values melted away
as by magic — Satanic magic, the poor lambs
thought. All stocks looked "sick," looked as
though prices would go much lower; murmurs of
worse things to come were in the air, vague, dis-
quieting, ruin-breeding. The atmosphere of the

Street was supersaturated with apprehension, and
the black shadow of Panic brooded over the Stock
Exchange, chilling the little gamblers' hearts, wip-
ing out the last of the little gamblers' margins.
And even the presidents of the solid, conservative
banks studied the ticker uneasily in their offices.

Greenbaum was promptly admitted to Sharpe's
private office.   It was a half-darkened room, the
windows having wire-screens, summer and winter,
in order that prying eyes across the street might not
see his visitors or his confidential brokers, whose
identity it was advisable should remain unknown
to the Street.   He was walking up and down the
room, pausing from time to time to look at the
tape.   The ticker is the only telescope the stock-
market general has; it tells him what his forces
are doing and how the enemy is meeting his attacks.   Every inch of the tape is so much ground;
every quotation represents so many shots.

There was something feline in Sharpe's stealthy,
soundless steps, in his mustaches, in the conforma-
tion of his face — broad of forehead and triangu-
lating chinward.   In his eyes, too, there was something tigerish — unmelodramatically cold hearted
and coldly curious as they looked upon Mr. Jacob
Greenbaum.   Unconsciously the unfanciful Trust-
maker asked himself whether Sharpe's heart-beats

were not ticker ticks, impassively indicating the pulse of the stock-market.

"Hallo, Greenbaum."

"How do you do, Mr. Sharpe?" quoth the millionaire senior partner of the firm of Greenbaum, Lazarus & Co. "I hope you are well?" He bent his head to one side, his eyes full of a caressing scrutiny, as though to ascertain the exact condition of Sharpe's health. "Yes, you must be. I haven't seen you look so fine in a long time."

"You didn't come up here just to tell me this, Greenbaum, did you? How's your Turpentine? Oh!" — with a long whistle — "I see. You want me to go into it, hey?" And he laughed — a sort of half-chuckle, half-snarl.

Greenbaum looked at him admiringly; then, with a tentative smile, he said: "I am discovered!"

Nearly every American may be met as an equal on the field of Humor. To jest in business matters of the greatest importance bespoke the national trait. Moreover, if Sharpe declined, Greenbaum could treat the entire affair — the proposal and the rejection — as parts of a joke.

"Well?" said Sharpe, unhumorously.

"What's the matter with a pool?"

"How big?" coldly.

"Up to the limit." Again the Trust-maker smiled, uncertainly.

"You haven't all the capital stock, I hope."

"Well, call it 100,000 shares," said Greenbaum, more uncertainly and less jovially.

"Who is to be in it besides you?"

"Oh, you know; the same old crowd."

"Oh, I know," mimicked Mr. Sharpe, scornfully, "the same old crowd. You ought to have come to me before; it will take something to overcome your own reputations. How much will each take?"

"We'll fix that O. K. if you take hold," answered Greenbaum, laughingly. "We've got over 100,000 shares and we'd rather some one else held some of it. We ain't hogs. Ha! Ha!"

"But, the distillers?"

"They are in the pool. I've got most of their stock in my office. I'll see that it does not come out until I say so."

There was a pause. Between Sharpe's eyebrows were two deep lines. At length, he said:

"Bring your friends here, this afternoon. Goodby, Greenbaum. And, I say, Greenbaum."

"Yes?"

"No funny tricks at any stage of the game."

"What's the use of saying such things, Mr. Sharpe?" with an experimental frown.

"The use is so you won't try any. Come at four," and Mr. Sharpe began to pace up and down the room. Greenbaum hesitated, still frowning tentatively; but he said nothing and at length went out.

Sharpe looked at the tape. "Turp" was $29\frac{1}{4}$.

He resumed his restless march back and forth. It was only when the market "went against him" that Mr. Sharpe did not pace about the room in the mechanical way of a menagerie animal, glancing everywhere but seeing nothing. When something unexpected happened in the market Sharpe stood immobile beside the ticker, because his overworked nerves were tense — like a tiger into whose cage there enters a strange and eatable animal.

On the minute of four there called on Mr. Sharpe the senior partners of the firms of Greenbaum, Lazarus & Co., I. & S. Wechsler, Morris Steinfelder's Sons, Reis & Stern, Kohn, Fischel & Co., Silberman & Lindheim, Rosenthal, Shaffran & Co., and Zeman Bros.

They were ushered not into the private office, but into a sumptuously furnished room, the walls of which were covered with dashing oil paintings of horses and horse-races. The visitors seated themselves about a long oaken table.

Mr. Sharpe appeared at the threshold.

"How do you do, gentlemen? Don't move, please; don't move." He made no motion to shake hands with any of them, but Greenbaum came to him and held out his fat dexter resolutely and Sharpe took it. Then Greenbaum sat down and said, "We're here," and smiled, blandly.

Sharpe stood at the head of the polished, shining table, and glanced slowly down the double row of alert faces. His look rested a fraction of a minute on each man's eyes — a sharp, half-contemptuous, almost menacing look that made the older men uncomfortable and the younger resentful.

"Greenbaum tells me you wish to pool your Turpentine stock and have me market it for you."

All nodded; a few said "yes"; one — Lindheim, *aetat* 27 — said, flippantly, "That's what."

"Very well. What will each man's proportion be?"

"I have a list here, Sharpe," put in Greenbaum. He intentionally omitted the "Mr." for effect upon his colleagues. Sharpe noted it, but did not mind it.

Sharpe read aloud:

Greenbaum, Lazarus & Co	38,000	shares.
I. & S. Wechsler	14,000	"
Morris Steinfelder's Sons	14,000	"
Reis & Stern	11,000	"
Kohn, Fischel & Co	10,000	"
Silberman & Lindheim	9,000	"
Rosenthal, Shaffran & Co	9,800	"
Zeman Bros	8,600	"
Total	114,400	shares.

"Is that correct, gentlemen?" asked Sharpe.

Greenbaum nodded his head and smiled affably as befitted the holder of the biggest block. Some said "Yes"; others, "That is correct." Young Lindheim said, "That's what." The founders of the firm — his uncle and his father — were dead, and he had inherited the entire business from the two. His flippancy was not inherited from either.

"It is understood," said Sharpe, slowly, "that I am to have complete charge of the pool, and conduct operations as I see fit. I want no advice and no questions. If there is any asking to be done, I'll do it. If my way does not suit you we'll call the deal off right here, because it's the only way I have. I know my business, and if you know yours you'll keep your mouths shut in this office and out of it."

No one said a word, not even Lindheim.

" Each of you will continue to carry the stock for which he has agreed to stand in the pool. You've had it a year and couldn't sell it, and you might keep it a few weeks more, until I sell it for you. It must be subject to my call at one minute's notice. I've looked into the company's business, and I think the stock can easily sell at 75 or 80."

" Something like a gasp of astonishment came from those eight hardened speculators. Then Greenbaum smiled, knowingly, as if that were *his* programme, memorized and spoken by Sharpe.

"It is also understood," went on Sharpe, very calmly, "that none of you has any other stock for sale at any price, excepting his proportion in this pool, and that proportion, of course, is not to be sold excepting by me." No one said a word, and he continued:

"My profit will be 25 per cent of the pool's winnings, figuring on the stock having been put in at 29. The remaining profits will be divided pro rata among you; the necessary expenses will be shared similarly. I think that's all. And, gentlemen, no unloading on the sly — not one share."

"I want you to understand, Mr. Sharpe, that

we are not in the habit of—" began Greenbaum
with perfunctory dignity. He felt it was his
duty to remonstrate before his colleagues.

"Oh, that's all right, Greenbaum. I know
you. That's why I'm particular. We've all
been in Wall Street more than a month or two.
I simply said, 'No shenanigan.' And, Greenbaum," he added, very distinctly, while his eyes
took on that curious, cold, menacing look, "I
mean it, every d——d word of it. I want the
numbers of all your stock-certificates. Excuse
me, gentlemen. I am very busy. Good-after-
noon."

And that is how the famous bull pool in
Turpentine came to be formed. They thought he
might have been nicer, more diplomatic; but as
they had sought him, not he them, they bore
with his eccentricities. Each pool manager had
his way, just as there are various kinds of
pools.

"Sam is not half a bad fellow," Greenbaum told
them, as if apologizing for a dear friend's weak-
nesses. "He wants to make out he is a devil of a
cynic, but he's all right. If you humor him you
can make him do anything. *I* always let him
have his way."

On the very next day began the historical ad-

vance in Turpentine.   It opened up at 30.   The
specialists — brokers who made a specialty of dealing in it — took 16,000 shares, causing an advance
to 32⅛.   Everybody who had been "landed" with
the shares at higher figures, and had bitterly re-
gretted it ever since, now began to feel hopeful.
As never before a stock had been manipulated,
with intent to deceive and malice prepense, so did
Sharpe manipulate Turpentine stock.   The tape
told the most wonderful stories in the world, not
the less wonderful because utterly untrue.   Thus,
one day the leading commission houses in the Street
were the buyers, which inevitably led to talk of
"important developments"; and the next day
brokers identified with certain prominent financiers
took calmly, deliberately, nonchalantly, all the
offerings; which clearly indicated that the afore-
mentioned financiers had acquired a "controlling
interest" — the majority of the stock — of the
American Turpentine Company.   And on another
day there was a long string of purchases of "odd"
lots — amounts less than 100 shares — by brokers
that usually did business for the Greenbaum syndicate, meaning that friends of the syndicate had
received a "tip" straight from "the inside" and
were buying for investment.

Then, one fine, sunshiny day, when everybody felt

very well and the general market was particularly
firm, the loquacious tape told the watchful professional gamblers of Wall Street — oh, so plainly!
— that there was "inside realizing"; said, almost
articulately to them, that the people most familiar
with the property were unloading.   Sharpe was
selling, with intentional clumsiness, stock he had
been forced to accumulate during his bull manipulation — for in order to advance the price he
had to buy much — and he was not averse to conveying such impressions as would lead to the
creation of a short interest, large enough to make
it profitable to "squeeze."   He had too much
company on the bull side.   And sure enough the
professional gamblers said: "Aha! They are
through with it.   The movement is over!" and
sold "Turp" short confidently, for a worthless
stock had no business to be selling at $46 a share.
The price yielded and they sold more the next
day.   But lo, on the day following, the Board
member of a very conservative house went into
the "Turp" crowd and bought it — he did not
"bid up" the price at all, but bought and bought
until he had accumulated 20,000 shares, and the
bears became panic-stricken, and rumors of a
near-by dividend began to circulate, and the bears
covered their shorts at a loss and "went long" —

bought in the hope of a further rise — and the
stock closed at 52.

And Sharpe reduced very greatly the amount
of "Turp" stock he had been obliged to take for
manipulative purposes. So far he was buying
more than he sold. Later he would sell more
than he bought. When the demand exceeds the
vendible supply, obviously the price rises; when
the supply for sale exceeds the demand, a fall re-
sults. But the average selling price of a big line
may be high enough to make the operation profitable, even though a decline occurs during the
course of the selling.

For a week "Turp" rested; then it began to
rise once more. At 56 and 58 it became the
most active stock of the entire list. Everybody
talked about it. The newspapers began to pub-
lish statements of the company's wonderful earnings, and the Street began to think that, in
common with other "trusts," the American Turpentine Company must be a very prosperous con-
cern. The company at this time developed a
habit of advancing prices a fraction of a cent per
gallon every week, so that the papers could talk
of the boom in the turpentine trade.

At 60 the Street thought there really must be
something behind the movement, for no mere

manipulation could put up the price thirty points
in a month's time, which shows what a wonderful
artist Sharpe was. And people began to look
curiously and admiringly and enviously and in
many other ways at "Jakey" Greenbaum and
his accomplices, and to accuse them of having intentionally kept down the price of the stock for
a year in order to "freeze out" the poor, unso-
phisticated stockholders, and to "tire out" some
of the early buyers, because "Turp," being "a
good thing," Greenbaum *et al.* wanted it all for
themselves. And Greenbaum *et al.* smiled guilt-
ily and said nothing, though Jakey winked
from time to time when they spoke to him about
it ; and old Isidore Wechsler cultivated a Napoleon III. look of devilish astuteness ; and "Bob"
Lindheim became almost dignified ; and myopic
little Morris Steinfelder gained 15 pounds and
Rosenthal stopped patting everybody on the
back, and mutely invited everybody to pat him
on the back.

Then Sharpe sent for "Jakey," and on the
next day young "Eddie" Lazarus swaggeringly
offered to wager $10,000 against $5,000 that a
dividend on "Turp" stock would be declared
during the year. Whereupon the newspapers of
their own accord began to guess how great a divi-

dend would be paid, and when; and various figures were mentioned in the Board room by brokers who confided to their hearers that they "got it on the dead q. t., *straight from the inside.*" And two days later Sharpe's unsuspected brokers offered to pay $1\frac{3}{4}$ per cent for the dividend on 100,000 shares, said dividend to be declared within sixty days or the money forfeited. And the stock sold up to $66\frac{3}{4}$, and the public wanted it. A big, broad market had been established, in which one could buy or sell the stock with ease by the tens of thousands of shares. The 114,400 shares, which at the inception of the movement at the unsalable price of $30 a share represented a theoretical $3,432,000, now readily vendible at $65 a share, meant $7,422,000; not half bad for a few weeks' work.

And still Sharpe, wonderful man that he was, gave no sign that he was about to begin unloading. Whereupon the other members of the pool began to wish he were not quite so greedy. They were satisfied to quit, they said. The presence of the pool's stock in their offices began to irritate them. They knew the vicissitudes of life, the uncertainties of politics, and of the stock market. Supposing some crazy anarchist blew up the President of the United States, or the

Emperor of Germany were to insult his grand-
mother, the market would " break " to pieces, and
their $4,000,000 of paper profits would disap-
pear. They implored, individually and collec-
tively, Mr. Jacob Greenbaum to call on Sharpe ;
and Greenbaum, disregarding a still, small voice
that warned him against it, went to Sharpe's
office, and came out of it, two minutes later,
somewhat flushed, and assured his colleagues one
by one that Sharpe was all right, and that he
seemed to know his business. Also, that he was
cranky that day. He always was, added Greenbaum forgivingly, when one of his horses lost a
race.

The stock fluctuated between 60 and 65. It
seemed to be having a resting spell. But as it
had enjoyed these periods of repose on three several occasions during the rise — at 40 and 48 and
56 — the public became all the more eager to buy
it whenever it fell to 60 or 59, for the Street was
now full of tips that "Turp" would go to par.
And such was the public's speculative temper and
Mr. Sharpe's good work that disinterested observers were convinced the stock would surely sell
above 90 at the very least. Mr. Sharpe still
bought and sold, but he sold twice as much as
he bought, and the big block he had been obliged

to take in the course of his manipulation diminished.   On the next day he hoped to begin selling the pool stock.

That very day Mr. Greenbaum, as he returned to his office from his luncheon, felt well pleased with the meal and therefore with himself and therefore with everything.   He scanned a yard or two of the tape and smiled.   "Turp" was certainly very active and very strong.

"In such a market," thought Mr. Greenbaum, "Sharpe can't possibly tell he's getting stock from me.   In order to be on the safe side I'm going to let him have a couple of thousand.   Then, should anything happen, I'd be that much ahead. Ike!" he called to a clerk.

"Yes, sir."

"Sell two — wait; make it 3,000 — no, never mind.   Send for Mr. Ed Lazarus."   And he muttered to himself, with a subthrill of pleasure : "I can just as well as not make it 5,000 shares."

"Eddie," he said to his partner's son, "give an order to some of the room traders, say to Willie Schiff, to sell five — er — six — tell him to sell 7,000 shares of Turpentine and to borrow the stock.   I am not selling a share, see?" with a wink.   "It's short selling by him, do you understand?"

"Do I? Well, I guess. I'll fix that part O.K.," said young Lazarus, complacently. He thought he would cover Greenbaum's tracks so well as to deceive everybody, including that highly disagreeable man, Samuel Wimbleton Sharpe. He felt so confident, so elated, did the young man, that when he gave the order to his friend and club-mate, Willie Schiff, he raised it to 10,000 shares. Greenbaum's breach of faith had grown from the relatively small lot of 2,000 shares to five times that amount. It was to all appearances short stock, and it was duly "borrowed" by young Schiff. It was advisable that it should so appear. In the first place no member of the pool could supply the stock which he held, because Sharpe could trace the selling to the office, as he had the numbers of the stock certificates. And, again, short selling does not have the weakening effect that long selling has. When stock is sold short it is evident that sooner or later the seller will have to buy it back; that is, a future demand for the stock is assured from this source, if from no other. Whereas, long stock is that actually held by some one.

Isidore Wechsler, who held 14,000 shares, was suffering from a bad liver the same day that Greenbaum was suffering from nothing at all, not

even a conscience.   A famous art collection would
be sold at auction that week, and he felt sure his
vulgar friend, " Abe " Wolff, would buy a couple
of exceptionally fine Troyons and a world-famous
Corot, merely to get his name in the papers.

" 'Turp,' 62⅞," said his nephew, who was standing by the ticker.

Then old Wechsler had an idea.   If he sold
2,000 shares of Turpentine at 62 or 63, he would
have enough to buy the best ten canvases of the
collection.   His name — and the amounts paid —
would grace the columns of the papers.   What
was 3,000 shares, or even 4,000, when Sharpe had
made such a big, broad market for the stock ?

" Why, I might as well make it 5,000 shares
while I'm about it, for there's no telling what may
happen if Sharpe should overstay his market.
I'll build a new stable at Westhurst "—his country place — " and call it," said old Wechsler to
himself, in his peculiar, facetious way so renowned
in Wall Street, " the Turpentine Horse Hotel, in
honor of Sharpe."   And so his 5,000 shares were
sold by E. Halford, who had the order from Her-
zog, Wertheim & Co., who received it from Wechsler.   It was short selling, of course.

Total breach of faith, 15,000 shares.

Now that very evening Bob Lindheim's ex-

tremely handsome wife wanted a necklace, and
wanted it at once; also she wanted it of filbert-sized
diamonds. She had heard her husband speak
highly of Sam Sharpe's masterly manipulation of
Turpentine, and she knew he was "in on the
ground floor." She read the newspapers, and she
always followed the stock market diligently, for
Bob, being young and loving, used to give her a
share in his stock deals from time to time, and
she learned to figure for herself her "paper" or
theoretical profits, when there were any, so that
Bob couldn't have "welched" if he had wished.
On this particular evening she had statistics ready
for him, showing how much money he had made;
and she wanted that necklace. She had longed
for it for months. It cost only $17,000. But
there was also a lovely bracelet, diamonds and
rubies, and ——

Lindheim, to his everlasting credit, remonstrated and told her: "Wait until the pool real-
izes, sweetheart. I don't know at what price that
will be, for Sharpe says nothing. But I know
we'll all make something handsome, and so will
you. I'll give you 500 shares at 30. There!"

"But I want it now!" she protested, pouting.
She was certainly beautiful, and when she pouted,
with her rich, red lips ——

" Wait a week, dear," he urged nevertheless.

" Lend me the money now, and I'll pay it back to you when you give me what I make on the deal," she said, with fine finality.   And seeing hesitation in Bob's face, she added, solemnly : " Honest, I will, Bob.   I'll pay you back every cent, this time."

" I'll think about it," said Bob.   He always said it when he had capitulated, and she knew it, and so she said, magnanimously : " Very well, dear."

Lindheim thought 1,000 shares would do it, so he decided to sell a thousand the next day, for you can never tell what may happen, and accidents seldom help the bulls.   But as he thought of it in his office more calmly, more deliberately, away from his wife and from the influence she exercised over him, it struck him forcibly that it was wrong to sell 1,000 shares of Turpentine stock. He might as well as not make it 2,500 ; and he did.   He was really a modest fellow, and very young.   His wife's cousin sold the stock for him, apparently short.

Total breach of faith, 17,500 shares.   The market stood it well.   Sharpe was certainly a wonderful chap.

Unfortunately, Morris Steinfelder, Jr., decided

to sell 1,500 "Turp," and did so. The stock actually rose a half point on his sales. So he sold another 1,500, and, as a sort of parting shot, 500 shares more. All this through an unsuspected broker.

Total breach of faith, 21,000 shares. The market was but slightly affected.

Then Louis Reis of Reis & Stern, "Andy" Fischel of Kohn, Fischel & Co., Hugo Zeman of Zeman Bros., and "Joe" Shaffran of Rosenthal, Shaffran & Co., all thought they could break their pledges to Sharpe with impunity, and each sold, to be on the safe side. This last lump figured up as follows :

	Sales First Contemplated.	Period of Hesitancy.	Actual Sales.
	Shares.	Minutes.	Shares.
Louis Reis....................	1,500	3	2,600
Andy Fischel..............	2,000	15	5,000
Hugo Zeman................	1,000	0	1,000
Joe Shaffran................	500	$1\frac{3}{4}$	1,800

Total breach of faith, 31,400 shares.

The market did not take it well. Sharpe, endeavoring to realize on the remainder of his manipulative purchases, found that "some one had been there before him."

An accurate list of the buyers and sellers was
sent in every day by his lieutenants, for all but
the most skilful operators invariably betray themselves when they attempt to sell a big block of
stock. He scanned it very carefully now, and
put two and two together; and he made certain
inquiries and put four and four together — four
names and four other names. He saw through
the time-worn device of the fictitious short selling.
He knew the only people who would dare sell
such a large amount must be his colleagues. He
also was convinced that their breach of faith was
not a concerted effort, because if they had discussed the matter they would have sold a smaller
quantity. He knew where nearly every share of
the stock was. It was his business to know everything about it.

"Two," he said to his secretary, "may play at
that game." And he began to play.

By seemingly reckless, plunging purchases he
started the stock rushing upward with a vengeance
—63, 64, 65, 66, four points in as many minutes. The floor of the Stock Exchange was the
scene of the wildest excitement. The market —
why, the market was simply Turpentine. Everybody was buying it, and everybody was wonder-
ing how high it would go, Greenbaum and the

other seven included. It looked as if the stock
had resumed its triumphant march to par.

Then Sharpe called in all the stock his brokers
were loaning to the shorts, and he himself began
to borrow it. This, together with the legitimate
requirements of the big short interest, created a
demand so greatly in excess of the supply that
Turpentine loaned at a sixty-fourth, at a thirty-
second, at an eighth, and finally at a quarter pre-
mium over night. It meant that the shorts had
either to cover or to pay $25 per diem for the
use of each 100 shares of stock they borrowed.
On the 31,400 shares that the syndicate was bor-
rowing it meant an expense of nearly $8,000 a
day; and in addition the stock was rising in
price. The shorts were losing at the rate of
many thousands a minute. There was no telling
where the end would be, but it certainly looked
stormy for both the real and the fictitious shorts.

Mr. Sharpe sent a peremptory message to
Greenbaum, Lazarus & Co.; I. & M. Wechsler;
Morris Steinfelder's Sons; Reis & Stern; Kohn,
Fischel & Co.; Silberman & Lindheim; Rosen-
thal, Shaffran & Co.; and Zeman Bros. It was
the same message to all:

"*Send me at once all your Turpentine stock!*"

There was consternation and dismay, also ad-

miration and self-congratulation, among the re-
cipients of the message.   They would have to buy
back in the open market the stock they had sold
a few days before.   It would mean losses on the
treasonable transactions of fully a quarter of a
million, but the pool " stood to win " simply fab-
ulous sums, if Mr. Sharpe did his duty.

There were some large blocks of stock for sale
at 66, but Sharpe's brokers cleared the figures
with a fierce, irresistible rush, whooping exultantly.   The genuine short interest was simply panic-
stricken, and atop it all there came orders to buy
an aggregate of 31,400 shares — orders from
Messrs. Greenbaum, Wechsler, Lindheim, Steinfelder, Reis, Fischel, Shaffran, and Zeman.   The
stock rose grandly on their buying : 4,000 shares
at 66 ; 2,200 at 66$\frac{3}{8}$; 700 at 67$\frac{5}{8}$; 1,200 at 68 ;
3,200 at 69$\frac{1}{2}$; 2,000 at 70 ; 5,700 at 70$\frac{1}{2}$; 1,-
200 at 72.   Total, 31,400 shares bought in by
the " Skindicate."   Total, 31,400 shares sold by
Samuel Wimbleton Sharpe to his own associates
in the great Turpentine pool.   In all he found
buyers for 41,700 shares that day, but it had
taken purchases of exactly 21,100 to " stampede
the shorts " earlier in the day, and in addition he
held 17,800 shares acquired in the course of his
bull manipulation, which had not been disposed of

when he discovered the breach of faith, so that at
the day's close he found himself not only without
a share of stock manipulatively purchased, but
" short " for his personal account of 2,800 shares.

The newspapers published picturesque accounts
of the " Great Day in Turpentine." A powerful
clique, they said, owned so much of the stock
— had " cornered " it — that they could easily
mark up the price to any figure. They called it
a " memorable squeeze." It was hinted also that
Mr. Sharpe had been on the wrong side of the
market, and one paper gave a wealth of details
and statistics in bold, bad type to prove that the
wily bear leader had been caught short of 75,000
shares, and had covered at a loss of $1,500,000.
A newspaper man whose relations with Sharpe
were intimate asked him, very carelessly : " What
the deuce caused the rise in Turpentine ? " and
Sharpe drawled : " I don't know for a certainty,
but I rather imagine it was inside buying ! "

On the next day came the second chapter of
the big Turpentine deal. Mr. Sharpe, having received the pool's 114,400 shares, divided it into
three lots, 40,000 shares, 50,000 shares, and 24,-
400 shares. The market had held fairly strong,
but the lynx-eyed room traders failed to perceive
the usual " support " in " Turp " and began to

sell it in order to make sure. There was enough
commission-house buying and belated short-
covering to keep it moderately steady. Then the
room traders redoubled their efforts to depress it,
by selling more than there were buying orders
for; also by selling it cheaper than was warranted
by the legitimate demand for the stock. It was
a favorite trick to offer to sell thousands of shares
lower than people were willing to pay, in order to
frighten the timid holders and make them sell;
which in turn would make still others sell, until
the movement became general enough to cause a
substantial fall.

Slowly the price began to yield. All that was
needed was a leader. Whereupon Mr. Sharpe
took the first lot of pool stock, 40,000 shares,
and hurled it full at the market. The impact was
terrible; the execution appalling. The market
reeled crazily. The stock, which after selling up
to $72\frac{3}{4}$ had "closed" on the previous day at $71\frac{7}{8}$,
dropped twenty points and closed at 54. The
newspapers said that the corner was "busted";
that the "squeeze" was over. Hundreds of people
slept ill that night. Scores did not sleep at all.

On the next day he fired by volleys 50,000
shares more at the market. The stock sank to
$41\frac{1}{4}$. Such a break was almost unprecedented.

The Street asked itself if it were not on the eve
of a crash that would become historic in a district
whose chronology is reckoned by big market
movements.

Greenbaum rushed to Sharpe's office. The terrible break gave him courage to do anything. A
Wall Street worm will turn when the market
misbehaves itself.

"What's the matter?" he asked angrily.
"What are you doing to Turpentine?"

Sharpe looked him full in the face, but his
voice was even and emotionless as he replied:
"Somebody has been selling on us. I don't know
who. I wish I did. I was afraid I might have
to take 100,000 shares more, so I just sold as
much as I could. I've marketed most of the
pool's stock. If it had not been for the jag of
stock I struck around 60 and 62, Turpentine
would be selling at 85 or 90 to-day. Come
again next week, Greenbaum; and keep cool.
Did you ever know me to fail? Good-by, Greenbaum; and don't raise your voice when you speak
to me."

"This has gone too far," said Greenbaum,
hotly. "You must give me an explanation or by
Heaven I'll —— "

"Greenbaum," said Mr. Sharpe, in a listless

voice, "don't get excited. Good-by, Greenbaum.
Be virtuous and you will be happy." And he
resumed his caged-tiger pacing up and down his
office. As by magic, Mr. Sharpe's burly private
secretary appeared, and said: "This way, Mr.
Greenbaum," and led the dazed Trust-maker from
the office. On his return Sharpe told him:
" There is no need to accuse those fellows of
breach of faith. They'd deny it."

The next day Mr. Sharpe simply poured the
remaining 25,000 shares of the pool's stock on
the market as one pours water from a pitcher into
a cup. The bears had it all their own way. The
loquacious tape said, ever so plainly: "This is
nothing but inside liquidation, all the more
dangerous and ominous since it is at such low
figures and is so urgent in its character. Heaven
alone can tell where it will end; and there is no
telephone communication thither."

Everybody was selling because somebody had
started a rumor that the courts had dissolved the
company for gross violation of the Anti-Trust
law, and that a receiver had been appointed.
Having sold out the last of the pool's stock, Mr.
Sharpe "took in" at $22 a share the 2,800 shares
which he had put out at $72, a total profit on
his small "line" of $140,000.

Turpentine stock had declined fifty points in fifteen business hours. It meant a shrinkage in the market value of the company's capital stock of $15,000,000. The shrinkage in the self-esteem of some of the pool was measurable only in billions.

Sharpe notified his associates that the pool had completely realized — *i.e.*, had sold out — and that he would be pleased to meet them at his office on Monday — this was Thursday — at eleven A.M., when he would have checks and an accounting ready for them. He refused himself to Greenbaum, Wechsler, Zeman, Shaffran, and others who called to see what could be done to save their reputations from the wreck of Turpentine. The stalwart private secretary told them that Mr. Sharpe was out of town. He was a very polite man, was the secretary; and an amateur boxer of great proficiency.

Failing to find Sharpe, they hastily organized a new pool, of a self-protective character, and sent in "supporting" orders. They were obliged to take large quantities of stock that day and the next in order to prevent a worse smash, which would hurt them in other directions. They found themselves with more than 50,000 shares on their hands, and the price was only 26 @ 28. And

merely to try to sell the stock at that time
threatened to start a fresh Turpentine panic.

They met Sharpe on Monday. His speech was
not so short as usual. He had previously sent to
each man an envelope containing a check and a
statement, and now he said, in a matter-of-fact
tone:

"Gentlemen and Greenbaum, you all know
what I did for Turpentine on the up-tack.
Around 62 I began to strike some stock which I
couldn't account for. I knew none of you had
any for sale, of course, as you had pledged me
your honorable words not to sell, save through
me. But the stock kept coming out, even though
the sellers borrowed against it, as if it were short
stock, and I began to fear I had met an inex-
haustible supply. It is always best on such
occasions to act promptly, and so, after driving in
the real shorts, I sold out our stock. The average
selling price was 40. If it had not been for that
mysterious selling it would have been 80. After
commissions and other legitimate pool expenses, I
find we have made nine points net, or $1,029,600,
of which 25 per cent., or $250,000, come to me
according to the agreement. It is too bad some
people didn't know enough to hold their stock for
90. But I find Wall Street is full of uncertain-

ties — there is so much stupidity in the district.
I trust you are satisfied. In view of the circumstances, I am. Yes, indeed. Good-day, gentlemen; and you too, Greenbaum, good-day.'

There was nothing tigerish about him. He
was affable and polished; they could see that he
seemed pleased to the purring point. He nodded
to them and went into his inner office.

They blustered and fumed among themselves
and gained courage thereby and tried Sharpe's
door and found it locked. They knocked thereon,
vehemently, and the ubiquitous private secretary
came out and told them that Mr. Sharpe had an
important engagement and could not be disturbed,
but that he was authorized to discuss any item of
the statement, and he had charge of all the
vouchers, in the shape of brokers' reports, etc.
So they expressed their opinions of the private
secretary and of his master rather mildly, and
went out, crestfallen. Outside they compared
notes, and in a burst of honesty they confessed.
Then, illogically enough, they cursed Sharpe.
The pool was not "ahead of the game." They
had so much more stock on their hands than they
desired, that in reality they were heavy losers!

And as time wore on they had to buy more
" Turp"; and more " Turp"; and still more

"Turp." They thought they could emulate Sharpe and rush the price up irresistibly, at any rate up to 50. They declared a dividend of 2 per cent on the stock. But they could not market Turpentine. Again and again they tried, and again and again they failed. And each time the failure was worse because they had to take more stock.

It is now quoted at 16 @ 18. But it is not readily vendible at that figure; nor, indeed, at any price. Opposition distilleries are starting up in all the turpentine districts, and the trade outlook is gloomy. And the principal owners of the stock of the American Turpentine Company, holding among them not less than **140,000** out of the entire issue of **300,000** unvendible shares, are the famous "Greenbaum Skindicate."

THE TIPSTER

THE TIPSTER

GILMARTIN was still laughing professionally at the prospective buyer's funny story when the telephone on his desk buzzed. He said : "Excuse me for a minute, old man," to the customer — Hopkins, the Connecticut manufacturer.

"Hello ; who is this ?" he spoke into the transmitter. "Oh, how are you ? —Yes — I was out — Is that so ? — Too bad — Too bad — Yes; just my luck to be out. I might have known it ! — Do you think so ? — Well, then, sell the 200 Occidental common — You know best — What about Trolley ? — Hold on ? — All right; just as you say — I hope so — I don't like to lose, and — Ha ! Ha ! — I guess so — Good-by."

"It's from my brokers," explained Gilmartin, hanging up the receiver. "I'd have saved five hundred dollars if I had been here at half-past ten. They called me up to advise me to sell out, and the price is off over three points. I could have got out at a profit, this morning ; but, no sir; not I. I had to be away, trying to buy some camphor."

Hopkins was impressed. Gilmartin perceived it and went on, with an air of comical wrath which

79

he thought was preferable to indifference: "It isn't the money I mind so much as the tough luck of it. I didn't make my trade in camphor after all and I lost in stocks, when if I'd only waited five minutes more in the office I'd have got the message from my brokers and saved my five hundred. Expensive, my time is, eh?" with a woful shake of the head.

"But you're ahead of the game, aren't you?" asked the customer, interestedly.

"Well, I guess yes. Just about twelve thousand."

That was more than Gilmartin had made; but having exaggerated, he immediately felt very kindly disposed toward the Connecticut man.

"Whew!" whistled Hopkins, admiringly. Gilmartin experienced a great tenderness toward him. The lie was made stingless by the customer's credulity. This brought a smile of subtle relief to Gilmartin's lips. He was a pleasant-faced, pleasant-voiced man of three-and-thirty. He exhaled health, contentment, neatness, and an easy conscience. Honesty and good-nature shone in his eyes. People liked to shake hands with him. It made his friends talk of his lucky star; and they envied him.

"I bought this yesterday for my wife; took it

out of a little deal in Trolley," he told Hopkins,
taking a small jewel-box from one of the desk's
drawers. It contained a diamond ring, somewhat
showy but obviously quite expensive. Hopkins'
semi-envious admiration made Gilmartin add,
genially: "What do you say to lunch? I feel I am
entitled to a glass of ' fizz ' to forget my bad luck
of this morning." Then, in an exaggeratedly
apologetic tone : " Nobody likes to lose five hundred dollars on an empty stomach ! "

"She'll be delighted, of course," said Hopkins,
thinking of Mrs. Gilmartin. Mrs. Hopkins loved
jewelry.

"She's the nicest little woman that ever lived.
Whatever is mine, is hers ; and what's hers is her
own. Ha! Ha! But," becoming nicely serious,
" all that I'll make out of the stock market I'm
going to put away for her, in her name. She can
take better care of it than I ; and, besides, she's
entitled to it, anyhow, for being so nice to me."

That is how he told what a good husband he
was. He felt so pleased over it, that he went on,
sincerely regretful: "She's visiting friends in
Pennsylvania or I'd ask you to dine with us."
And they went to a fashionable restaurant
together.

Day after day Gilmartin thought persistently

that Maiden Lane was too far from Wall Street.
There came a week in which he could have made
four very handsome " turns " had he but been in
the brokers' office.   He was out on business for
his firm and when he returned the opportunity
had gone, leaving behind it vivid visions of what
might have been ; also the conviction that time,
tide and the ticker wait for no man.   Instead of
buying and selling quinine and balsams and essen-
tial oils for Maxwell & Kip, drug brokers and im-
porters, he decided to make the buying and selling
of stocks and bonds his exclusive business.   The
hours were easy ; the profits would be great.   He
would make enough to live on.   He would not
let the Street take away what it had given.   That
was the great secret : to know when to quit !   He
would be content with a moderate amount, wisely
invested in gilt-edged bonds.   And then he would
bid the Street good-by forever.

Force of long business custom and the indefi-
nable fear of new ventures for a time fought successfully his increasing ticker-fever.   But one day
his brokers wished to speak to him, to urge him
to sell out his entire holdings, having been advised
of an epoch-making resolution by Congress.
They had received the news in advance from a
Washington customer.   Other brokers had im-

portant connections in the Capital and therefore
there was no time to lose. They dared not
assume the responsibility of selling him out without his permission. Five minutes — five eterni-
ties! — passed before they could talk by telephone with him; and when he gave his order to
sell, the market had broken five or six points.
The news was "out." The news-agencies' slips
were in the brokers' offices and half of Wall
Street knew. Instead of being among the first ten
sellers Gilmartin was among the second hundred.

II.

The clerks gave him a farewell dinner. All
were there, even the head office-boy to whom the
two-dollar subscription was no light matter. The
man who probably would succeed Gilmartin as
manager, Jenkins, acted as toastmaster. He
made a witty speech which ended with a neatly
turned compliment. Moreover, he seemed sincerely
sorry to bid good-by to the man whose departure
meant promotion — which was the nicest compliment of all. And the other clerks — old Williamson, long since ambition-proof; and young Hardy,
bitten ceaselessly by it; and middle-aged Jameson, who knew he could run the business much
better than Gilmartin; and Baldwin, who never

thought of business in or out of the office — all told him how good he had been and related corroborative anecdotes that made him blush and the others cheer ; and how sorry they were he would no longer be with them, but how glad he was going to do so much better by himself ; and they hoped he would not "cut" them when he met them after he had become a great millionaire. And Gilmartin felt his heart grow soft and feelings not all of happiness came over him. Danny, the dean of the office boys, whose surname was known only to the cashier, rose and said, in the tones of one speaking of a dear departed friend : "He was the best man in the place. He always was all right." Everybody laughed ; whereupon Danny went on, with a defiant glare at the others: "I'd work for him for nothin' if he'd want me, instead of gettin' ten a week from anyone else." And when they laughed the harder at this he said, stoutly : " Yes, I would ! " His eyes filled with tears at their incredulity, which he feared might be shared by Mr. Gilmartin. But the toastmaster rose very gravely and said : "What's the matter with Danny ? " And all shouted in unison : " He's all right ! " with a cordiality so heartfelt that Danny smiled and sat down, blushing happily. And crusty Jameson, who knew he could

run the business so much better than Gilmartin,
stood up — he was the last speaker — and began :
" In the ten years I've worked with Gilmartin,
we've had our differences and — well — I — well
— er — oh, DAMN IT ! " and walked quickly to
the head of the table and shook hands violently
with Gilmartin for fully a minute, while all the
others looked on in silence.

Gilmartin had been eager to go to Wall Street.
But this leave-taking made him sad. The old
Gilmartin who had worked with these men was
no more and the new Gilmartin felt sorry. He
had never stopped to think how much they cared
for him nor indeed how very much he cared for
them. He told them, very simply, he did not
expect ever again to spend such pleasant years
anywhere as at the old office ; and as for his
spells of ill-temper — oh, yes, they needn't shake
their heads ; he knew he often was irritable — he
had meant well and trusted they would forgive
him. If he had his life to live over again he
would try really to deserve all that they had said
of him on this evening. And he was very, very
sorry to leave them. " Very sorry, boys ; very
sorry. *Very* sorry ! " he finished lamely, with a
wistful smile. He shook hands with each man —
a strong grip as though he were about to go on a

journey from which he might never return — and
in his heart of hearts there was a new doubt of
the wisdom of going to Wall Street. But it was
too late to draw back.

They escorted him to his house. They wished
to be with him to the last possible minute.

III.

Everybody in the drug trade seemed to think
that Gilmartin was on the high road to Fortune.
Those old business acquaintances and former com-
petitors whom he happened to meet in the street-
cars or in theatre lobbies always spoke to him
as to a millionaire-to-be, in what they imagined
was correct Wall Street jargon, to show him that
they too knew something of the great game. But
their efforts made him smile with a sense of su-
periority, at the same time that their admiration
for his cleverness and their good-natured envy for
his luck made his soul thrill joyously. Among
his new friends in Wall Street also he found much
to enjoy. The other customers — some of them
very wealthy men — listened to his views regarding the market as attentively as he, later, felt it
his polite duty to listen to theirs. The brokers
themselves treated him as a " good fellow." They
cajoled him into trading often — every one-hun-

dred shares he bought or sold meant $12.50 to
them — and when he won, they praised his un-
erring discernment. When he lost they soothed
him by scolding him for his recklessness — just as
a mother will treat her three-years-old's fall as a
great joke in order to deceive the child into
laughing at its misfortune. It was an average
office with an average clientele.

From ten to three they stood before the quotation board and watched a quick-witted boy chalk
the price-changes, which one or another of the
customers read aloud from the tape as it came
from the ticker. The higher stocks went the
more numerous the customers became, being al-
lured in great flocks to the Street by the tales of
their friends, who had profited greatly by the rise.
All were winning, for all were buying stocks in a
bull market. They resembled each other marvel-
lously, these men who differed so greatly in cast
of features and complexion and age. Life to all
of them was full of joy. The very ticker sounded
mirthful ; its clicking told of golden jokes. And
Gilmartin and the other customers laughed heart-
ily at the mildest of stories without even waiting
for the point of the joke. At times their fingers
clutched the air happily, as if they actually felt
the good money the ticker was presenting **to**

them. They were all neophytes at the great game — lambkins who were bleating blithely to inform the world what clever and formidable wolves they were. Some of them had sustained occasional losses; but these were trifling compared with their winnings.

When the slump came all were heavily committed to the bull side. It was a bad slump. It was so unexpected — by the lambs — that all of them said, very gravely, it came like a thunderclap out of a clear sky. While it lasted, that is, while the shearing of the flock was proceeding, it was very uncomfortable. Those same joyous, winning stock-gamblers, with beaming faces, of the week before, were fear-clutched, losing stock-gamblers, with livid faces, on what they afterward called the day of the panic. It really was only a slump; rather sharper than usual. Too many lambs had been over-speculating. The wholesale dealers in securities — and insecurities — held very little of their own wares, having sold them to the lambs, and wanted them back now — cheaper. The customers' eyes, as on happier days were intent on the quotation - board. Their dreams were rudely shattered; the fast horses some had all but bought joined the steam-yachts others almost had chartered. The beautiful homes

they had been building were torn down in the
twinkling of an eye. And the demolisher of
dreams and dwellings was the ticker, that instead
of golden jokes, was now clicking financial death.

They could not take their eyes from the board
before them. Their own ruin, told in mournful
numbers by the little machine, fascinated them.
To be sure, poor Gilmartin said : "I've changed
my mind about Newport. I guess I'll spend the
summer on my own *Hotel de Roof!*" And he
grinned ; but he grinned alone. Wilson, the dry
goods man, who laughed so joyously at everybody's jokes, was now watching, as if under a
hypnotic spell, the lips of the man who sat on
the high stool beside the ticker and called out the
prices to the quotation boy. Now and again
Wilson's own lips made curious grimaces, as if
speaking to himself. Brown, the slender, pale-
faced man, was outside in the hall, pacing to and
fro. All was lost, including honor. And he was
afraid to look at the ticker, afraid to hear the
prices shouted, yet hoping — for a miracle ! Gilmartin came out from the office, saw Brown and
said, with sickly bravado : "I held out as long as
I could. But they got *my* ducats. A sporting
life comes high, I tell you !" But Brown did not
heed him and Gilmartin pushed the elevator-

button impatiently and cursed at the delay. He
not only had lost the " paper " profits he had
accumulated during the bull-market but all his
savings of years had crumbled away beneath the
strokes of the ticker that day. It was the same
with all. They would not take a small loss at first
but had held on, in the hope of a recovery that
would " let them out even." And prices had sunk
and sunk until the loss was so great that it seemed
only proper to hold on, if need be a year, for
sooner or later prices must come back. But the
break " shook them out," and prices went just so
much lower because so many people had to sell,
whether they would or not.

IV.

After the slump most of the customers returned
to their legitimate business — sadder, but it is to
be feared, not much wiser men. Gilmartin, after
the first numbing shock, tried to learn of fresh
opportunities in the drug business. But his heart
was not in his search. There was the shame of
confessing defeat in Wall Street so soon after
leaving Maiden Lane ; but far stronger than this
was the effect of the poison of gambling. If it
was bad enough to be obliged to begin lower than
he had been at Maxwell & Kip's, it was worse to

condemn himself to long weary years of work in
the drug business when his reward, if he remained
strong and healthy, would consist merely in being
able to save a few thousands. But a few lucky
weeks in the stock market would win him back all
he had lost — and more !

He should have begun in a small way while he
was learning to speculate. He saw it now very
clearly. Every one of his mistakes had been due
to inexperience. He had imagined he knew the
market. But it was only now that he really knew
it and therefore it was only now, after the slump
had taught him so much, that he could reasonably
hope to succeed. His mind, brooding over his
losses, definitely dismissed as futile the resumption
of the purchase and sale of drugs, and dwelt persistently on the sudden acquisition of stock market
wisdom. Properly applied, this wisdom ought to
mean much to him. In a few weeks he was again
spending his days before the quotation board,
gossiping with those customers who had survived,
giving and receiving advice. And as time passed
the grip of Wall Street on his soul grew stronger
until it strangled all other aspirations. He could
talk, think, dream of nothing but stocks. He
could not read the newspapers without thinking
how the market would " take" the news contained

therein. If a huge refinery burnt down, with a loss to the "Trust" of $4,000,000, he sighed because he had not foreseen the catastrophe and had sold Sugar short. If a strike by the men of the Suburban Trolley Company led to violence and destruction of life and property, he cursed an unrelenting Fate because he had not had the prescience to "put out" a thousand shares of Trolley. And he constantly calculated to the last fraction of a point how much money he would have made if he had sold short just before the calamity at the very top prices and had covered his stock at the bottom. Had he only known! The atmosphere of the Street, the odor of speculation surrounded him on all sides, enveloped him like a fog, from which the things of the outside world appeared as though seen through a veil. He lived in the district where men do not say "Good-morning" on meeting one another, but "How's the market?" or, when one asks: "How do you feel?" receives for an answer: "Bullish!" or "Bearish!" instead of a reply regarding the state of health.

At first, after the fatal slump, Gilmartin importuned his brokers to let him speculate on credit, in a small way. They did. They were kindly enough men and sincerely wished to help him. But luck ran against him. With the obsti-

nacy of unsuperstitious gamblers he insisted on
fighting Fate. He was a bull in a bear market;
and the more he lost the more he thought the
inevitable "rally" in prices was due. He bought
in expectation of it and lost again and again, until
he owed the brokers a greater sum than he could
possibly pay; and they refused point blank to
give him credit for another cent, disregarding his
vehement entreaties to buy a last hundred, just
one more chance, the last, because he would be
sure to win. And, of course, the long-expected
happened and the market went up with a rapidity
that made the Street blink; and Gilmartin figured
that had not the brokers refused his last order, he
would have made enough to pay off the indebted-
ness and have left, in addition, $2,950; for he
would have "pyramided" on the way up. He
showed the brokers his figures, accusingly, and
they had some words about it and he left the
office, almost tempted to sue the firm for conspiracy with intent to defraud; but decided that
it was "another of Luck's sockdolagers" and let it
go at that, gambler-like.

When he returned to the brokers' office — the
next day — he began to speculate in the only way
he could — vicariously. Smith, for instance, who
was long of 500 St. Paul at 125, took less inter-

est in the deal than did Gilmartin who thenceforth
assiduously studied the news-slips and sought information on St. Paul all over the Street, listening thrillingly to tips and rumors regarding the
stock, suffering keenly when the price declined,
laughing and chirruping blithely if the quota-
tions moved upward, exactly as though it were
his own stock. In a measure it was as an ano-
dyne to his ticker-fever. Indeed, in some cases
his interest was so poignant and his advice so fre-
quent — he would speak of *our* deal — that the
lucky winner gave him a small share of his spoils,
which Gilmartin accepted without hesitation —
he was beyond pride-wounding by now — and
promptly used to back some miniature deal of his
own on the Consolidated Exchange or even in
"Percy's" — a dingy little bucket-shop, where
they took orders for two shares of stock on a
margin of one per cent.; that is, where a man
could bet as little as two dollars.

Later, it often came to pass that Gilmartin
would borrow a few dollars, when the customers
were not trading actively. The amounts he borrowed diminished by reason of the increasing fre-
quency of their refusals. Finally, he was asked
to stay away from the office where once he had
been an honored and pampered customer.

He became a Wall Street "has been" and
could be seen daily on New Street, back of the
Consolidated Exchange, where the "put" and
"call" brokers congregate. The tickers in the
saloons nearby fed his gambler's appetite. From
time to time luckier men took him into the same
be-tickered saloons, where he ate at the free lunch
counters and drank beer and talked stocks and
listened to the lucky winners' narratives with lips
tremulous with readiness to smile and grimace.
At times the gambler in him would assert itself
and he would tell the lucky winners, wrathfully,
how the stock he wished to buy but couldn't the
week before, had risen 18 points. But they,
saturated with their own ticker-fever, would nod
absently, their soul's eyes fixed on some quotation-
to-be ; or they would not nod at all but in their
eagerness to look at the tape from which they had
been absent two long minutes, would leave him
without a single word of consolation or even of
farewell.

V.

One day, in New Street, he overheard a very
well known broker tell another that Mr. Sharpe
was "going to move up Pennsylvania Central
right away." The over-hearing of the conversa-

tion was a bit of rare good luck that raised Gilmartin from his sodden apathy and made him
hasten to his brother-in-law who kept a grocery
store in Brooklyn.   He implored Griggs to go to
a broker and buy as much Pennsylvania Central
as he could — that is, if he wished to live in
luxury the rest of his life.   Sam Sharpe was going
to put it up.   Also, he borrowed ten dollars.

Griggs was tempted.   He debated with himself many hours, and at length yielded with mis-
givings.   He took his savings and bought one
hundred shares of Pennsylvania Central at 64 and
began to neglect his business in order to study
the financial pages of the newspapers.   Little by
little Gilmartin's whisper set in motion within
him the wheels of a ticker that printed on his
day-dreams the mark of the dollar.   His wife, seeing him preoccupied, thought business was bad ;
but Griggs denied it, confirming her worst fears.
Finally, he had a telephone put in his little shop,
to be able to talk to his brokers.

Gilmartin, with the ten dollars he had borrowed, promptly bought ten shares in a bucket
shop at $63\frac{7}{8}$; the stock promptly went to $62\frac{7}{8}$;
he was promptly " wiped " ; and the stock
promptly went back to $64\frac{1}{2}$.

On the next day a fellow-customer of the Gil-

martin of old days invited him to have a drink.
Gilmartin resented the man's evident prosperity.
He felt indignant at the ability of the other to
buy hundreds of shares. But the liquor soothed
him, and in a burst of mild remorse he told
Smithers, after an apprehensive look about him
as if he feared someone might overhear: "I'll
tell you something, on the dead q. t., for your
own benefit."

"Fire away!"

"Pa. Cent. is going 'way up."

"Yes?" said Smithers, calmly.

"Yes; it will cross par sure."

"Umph!" between munches of a pretzel.

"Yes. Sam Sharpe told"— Gilmartin was on
the point of saying a "friend of mine" but
caught himself and went on, impressively—"told
me, yesterday, to buy Pa. Cent. as he had accumulated his full line, and was ready to whoop it
up. And you know what Sharpe is," he finished,
as if he thought Smithers was familiar with
Sharpe's powers.

"Is that so?" nibbled Smithers.

"Why, when Sharpe makes up his mind to put
up a stock, as he intends to do with Pa. Cent.,
nothing on earth can stop him. He told me he
would make it cross par within sixty days. This

is no heresay, no tip. It's cold facts. I don't *hear* it's going up; I don't *think* it's going up; I *know* it's going up. Understand?" And he shook his right forefinger with a hammering motion.

In less than five minutes Smithers was so wrought up that he bought 500 shares and promised solemnly not to "take his profits," *i.e.* sell out, until Gilmartin said the word. Then they had another drink and another look at the ticker.

"You want to keep in touch with me," was Gilmartin's parting shot. "I'll tell you what Sharpe tells me. But you must keep it quiet," with a side-wise nod that pledged Smithers to honorable secrecy.

Had Gilmartin met Sharpe face to face, he would not have known who was before him.

Shortly after he left Smithers he buttonholed another acquaintance, a young man who thought he knew Wall Street, and therefore had a hobby — manipulation. No one could induce him to buy stocks by telling him how well the companies were doing, how bright the prospects, etc. That was bait for "suckers" not for clever young stock operators. But anyone, even a stranger, who said that "they" — the perennially mysterious "they,"

the "big men," the mighty "manipulators" whose
life was one prolonged conspiracy to pull the wool
over the public's eyes—"they" were going to
"jack up" these or the other shares, was wel-
comed, and his advice acted upon.   Young Freeman believed in nothing but "their" wickedness
and "their" power to advance or depress stock
values at will.   Thinking of his wisdom had given
him a chronic sneer.

"You're just the man I was looking for," said
Gilmartin, who hadn't thought of the young
man at all.

"Are you a deputy sheriff?"

"No."   A slight pause, for oratorical effect.
"I had a long talk with Sam to-day."

"What Sam?"

"Sharpe.   The old boy sent for me.   He was
in mighty good-humor too.   Tickled to death.
He might well be—he's got 60,000 shares of
Pennsylvania Central.   And there's going to be
from 50 to 60 points profit in it."

"H'm!" sniffed Freeman, skeptically, yet impressed by the change in Gilmartin's attitude
from the money-borrowing humility of the previous week to the confident tone of a man with a
straight tip.   Sharpe was notoriously kind to his
old friends—rich or poor.

"I was there when the papers were signed," Gilmartin said, hotly. "I was going to leave the room, but Sam told me I needn't. I can't tell you what it is about; really I can't. But he's simply going to put the stock above par. It's 64½ now, and you know and I know that by the time it is 75 the newspapers will all be talking about inside buying; and at 85 everybody will want to buy it on account of important developments; and at 95 there will be millions of bull tips on it and rumors of increased dividends, and people who would not look at it thirty points lower will rush in and buy it by the bushel. Let me know who is manipulating a stock, and to h — l with dividends and earnings. Them's *my* sentiments," with a final hammering nod, as if driving in a profound truth.

"Same here," assented Freeman, cordially. He was attacked on his vulnerable side.

Strange things happen in Wall Street. Sometimes tips come true. It so proved in this case. Sharpe started the stock upward brilliantly — the movement became historic in the Street — and Pa. Cent. soared dizzily and all the newspapers talked of it and the public went mad over it and it touched 80 and 85 and 88 and higher, and then Gilmartin made his brother-in-law sell out

and Smithers and Freeman. Their profits were :
Griggs, $3,000 ; Smithers, $15,100 ; Freeman,
$2,750. Gilmartin made them give him a good
percentage. He had no trouble with his brother-
in-law. Gilmartin told him it was an inviolable
Wall Street custom and so Griggs paid, with an
air of much experience in such matters. Freeman
was more or less grateful. But Smithers met
Gilmartin and full of his good luck repeated what
he had told a dozen men within the hour : "I did
a dandy stroke the other day. Pa. Cent. looked to
me like higher prices and I bought a wad of it.
I've cleaned up a tidy sum," and he looked proud
of his own penetration. He really had forgotten
that it was Gilmartin who had given him the tip.
But not so Gilmartin who retorted, witheringly :

"Well, I've often heard of folks that you put
into good things and they make money and afterward they come to you and tell how damned
smart they were to hit it right. But you can't
work that on me. I've got witnesses."

"Witnesses ? " echoed Smithers, looking cheap.
He remembered.

"Yes, wit-ness-es," mimicked Gilmartin,
scornfully. "I all but had to get on my knees
to make you buy it. And I told you when to
sell it, too. The information came to me straight

from headquarters and you got the use of it and now the least you can do is to give me twenty-five hundred dollars."

In the end he accepted $800. He told mutual friends that Smithers had cheated him.

VI.

It seemed as though the regeneration of Gilmartin had been achieved when he changed his shabby raiment for expensive clothes. He paid his tradesmen's bills and moved into better quarters. He spent his money as though he had made millions. One week after he had closed out the deal his friends would have sworn Gilmartin had always been prosperous. That was his exterior. His inner self remained the same — a gambler. He began to speculate again, in the office of Freeman's brokers.

At the end of the second month he had lost not only the $1,200 he had deposited with the firm, but an additional $250 he had given his wife and had been obliged to "borrow" back from her, despite her assurances that he would lose it. This time, the slump was really unexpected by all, even by the magnates — the mysterious and all powerful "they" of Freeman's — so that the loss of the second fortune did not reflect on Gilmartin's ability as a speculator but on his luck. As a matter of fact, he had been too careful and had sinned from over-timidity at first, only to plunge later and lose all.

As the result of much thought about his losses Gilmartin became a professional tipster. To let others speculate for him seemed the only sure way of winning. He began by advising ten victims — he learned in time to call them clients — to sell Steel Rod preferred, each man 100 shares; and to a second ten he urged the purchase of the same quantity of the same stock. To all he advised taking four points' profit. Not all followed his advice, but the seven clients who sold it made between them nearly $3,000 over night. His percentage amounted to $287.50. Six bought and when they lost he told them confidentially how the treachery of a leading member of the pool had obliged the pool managers to withdraw their support from the stock temporarily; whence the decline. They grumbled; but he assured them that he himself had lost nearly $1,600 of his own on account of the traitor.

For some months Gilmartin made a fair living but business became very dull. People learned to fight shy of his tips. The persuasiveness was gone from his inside news and from his confiden-

tial advice from Sharpe and from his beholding
with his own eyes the signing of epoch-making
documents. Had he been able to make his customers alternate their winnings and losses he
might have kept his trade. But for example,
" Dave " Rossiter, in Stuart & Stern's office, stu-
pidly received the wrong tip six times in succes-
sion. It wasn't Gilmartin's fault but Rossiter's
bad luck.

At length failing to get enough clients in the
ticker-district itself Gilmartin was forced to ad-
vertise in an afternoon paper, six times a week,
and in the Sunday edition of one of the leading
morning dailies. They ran like this :

WE MAKE MONEY

for our investors by the best system ever devised. Deal
with genuine experts. Two methods of operating ; one
speculative, the other insures absolute safety.

NOW

is the time to invest in a certain stock for ten points sure
profit. Three points margin will carry it. Remember how
correct we have been on other stocks. Take advantage
of this move.

IOWA MIDLAND.

Big movement coming in this stock. It's very near at hand.
Am waiting daily for word. Will get it in time. Splendid
opportunity to make big money. It costs only a 2-cent
stamp to write to me.

CONFIDENTIAL INFORMATION.

Private secretary of banker and stock operator of world-wide reputation, has valuable information. I don't wish your money. Use your own broker. All I want is a share of what you will surely make if you follow my advice.

WILL ADVANCE $40 PER SHARE.

A fortune to be made in a railroad stock. Deal pending which will advance same $40 per share within three months. Am in position to keep informed as to developments and the operations of a pool. Parties who will carry for me 100 shares with a New York Stock Exchange house will receive the full benefit of information. Investment safe and sure. Highest references given.

He prospered amazingly. Answers came to him from furniture dealers on Fourth Avenue and dairymen up the State and fruit growers in Delaware and factory workers in Massachusetts and electricians in New Jersey and coal miners in Pennsylvania and shop keepers and physicians and plumbers and undertakers in towns and cities near and far. Every morning Gilmartin telegraphed to scores of people — at their expense — to sell, and to scores of others to buy the same stocks. And he claimed his commissions from the winners.

Little by little his savings grew; and with them grew his desire to speculate on his own account. It made him irritable, not to gamble.

He met Freeman one day in one of his dissat-

isfied moods. Out of politeness he asked the
young cynic the universal query of the Street:

"What do you think of 'em?" He meant
stocks.

"What difference does it make what *I* think?"
sneered Freeman, with proud humility. "I'm
nobody." But he looked as if he did not agree
with himself.

"What do you *know*?" pursued Gilmartin,
mollifyingly.

"I know enough to be long of Gotham Gas.
I just bought a thousand shares at 180." He
really had bought a hundred only.

"What on?"

"On information. I got it straight from a
director of the company. Look here, Gilmartin,
I'm pledged to secrecy. But, for your own benefit, I'll just tell you to buy all the Gas you possibly can carry. The deal is on. I know that
certain papers were signed last night, and they
are almost ready to spring it on the public. They
haven't got all the stock they want. When they
get it, look out for fireworks."

Gilmartin did not perceive any resemblance between Freeman's tips and his own. He said, hesitatingly, as though ashamed of his timidity:

"The stock seems pretty high at 180."

" You won't think so when it sells at 250.
Gilmartin, I don't *hear* this ; I don't *think* it ; I
know it ! "

" All right ; I'm in," quoth Gilmartin, jovially.
He felt a sense of emancipation now that he had
made up his mind to resume his speculating. He
took every cent of the nine hundred dollars he
had made from telling people the same things
that Freeman told him now, and bought a hundred
Gotham Gas at $185 a share. Also he tele-
graphed to all his clients to plunge in the stock.

It fluctuated between 184 and 186 for a fort-
night. Freeman daily asseverated that "they"
were accumulating the stock. But, one fine day,
the directors met, agreed that business was bad
and having sold out most of their own holdings,
decided to reduce the dividend rate from 8 to 6
per cent. Gotham Gas broke seventeen points in
ten short minutes. Gilmartin lost all he had.
He found it impossible to pay for his advertise-
ments. The telegraph companies refused to accept any more "collect" messages. This de-
prived Gilmartin of his income as a tipster.
Griggs had kept on speculating and had lost all
his money and his wife's in a little deal in Iowa
Midland. All that Gilmartin could hope to get
from him was an occasional invitation to dinner.

Mrs. Gilmartin, after they were dispossessed for non-payment of rent, left her husband and went to live with a sister in Newark who did not like Gilmartin.

His clothes became shabby and his meals irregular. But always in his heart, as abiding as an inventor's faith in himself, there dwelt the hope that some day, somehow, he would "strike it rich" in the stock market.

One day he borrowed five dollars from a man who had made five thousand in Cosmopolitan Traction. The stock, the man said, had only begun to go up, and Gilmartin believed it and bought five shares in "Percy's," his favorite bucket-shop. The stock began to rise slowly but steadily. The next afternoon "Percy's" was raided, the proprietor having disagreed with the police as to price.

Gilmartin lingered about New Street, talking with other customers of the raided bucket shop, discussing whether or not it was a "put up job" of old Percy himself who, it was known, had been losing money to the crowd for weeks past. One by one the victims went away and at length Gilmartin left the ticker district. He walked slowly down Wall Street, then turned up William Street, thinking of his luck. Cosmopolitan Trac-

tion had certainly looked like higher prices. Indeed, it seemed to him that he could almost hear
the stock shouting, articulately: "*I'm going up,
right away, right away!*" If somebody would
buy a thousand shares and agree to give him the
profits on a hundred, on ten, on one!

But he had not even his carfare. Then he remembered that he had not eaten since breakfast.
It did him no good to remember it now. He
would have to get his dinner from Griggs in
Brooklyn.

"Why," Gilmartin told himself with a burst
of curious self-contempt, "I can't even buy a cup
of coffee!"

He raised his head and looked about him to
find how insignificant a restaurant it was in which
he could not buy even a cup of coffee. He had
reached Maiden Lane. As his glance ran up and
down the north side of that street, it was arrested
by the sign:

MAXWELL & KIP.

At first he felt but vaguely what it meant. It
had grown unfamiliar with absence. The clerks
were coming out. Jameson, looking crustier than
ever, as though he were forever thinking how
much better than Jenkins he could run the busi-

ness; Danny, some inches taller, no longer an office boy but spick and span in a blue serge suit and a necktie of the latest style, exhaling health and correctness; Williamson, grown very gray and showing on his face thirty years of routine; Baldwin, happy as of yore at the ending of the day's work, and smiling at the words of Jenkins — Gilmartin's successor who wore an air of authority, of the habit of command which he had not known in the old days.

Of a sudden Gilmartin was in the midst of his old life. He saw all that he had been, all that he might still be. And he was overwhelmed. He longed to rush to his old associates, to speak to them, to shake hands with them, to be the old Gilmartin. He was about to step toward Jenkins; but stopped abruptly. His clothes were shabby and he felt ashamed. But, he apologized to himself, he could tell them how he had made a hundred thousand and had lost it. And he even might borrow a few dollars from Jenkins.

Gilmartin turned on his heel with a sudden impulse and walked away from Maiden Lane quickly. All that he thought now was that he would not have them see him in his plight. He felt the shabbiness of his clothes without looking at them.

As he walked, a great sense of loneliness came over him.

He was back in Wall Street. At the head of the Street was old Trinity; to the right the sub-Treasury; to the left the Stock Exchange.

From Maiden Lane to the Lane of the Ticker — such had been his life.

"If I could only buy some Cosmopolitan Traction!" he said. Then he walked forlornly northward, to the great Bridge, on his way to Brooklyn to eat with Griggs, the ruined grocery-man.

A PHILANTHROPIC WHISPER

A PHILANTHROPIC WHISPER

THERE have been all manner of big stock operators and "leaders" in Wall Street — gentlemanly, well-educated leaders with a gift of epigram and foul-spoken leaders who knew as little of grammar as of manners; leaders to whom the stock market was only the Monte Carlo of the Tape and leaders to whom it was a means to an end; cool, calculating, steel-nerved leaders and fidgety, impulsive, excitable leaders; leaders who were church pillars and total abstainers and leaders whose only God was the ticker and whose most brilliant operations were carried on during the course of a drunken debauch. But never before, in the breathless history of Wall Street, had there been a leader whose following was numbered by the thousands and included not only the "shoe-string" speculators but the very richest of the rich! Never before a leader whose word took the place of statistical information, whose mere "I am buying it" created more purchasers for a stock than all the glowing prospectuses and all the accountants' affidavits and all the bankers' estimates.

At first Wall Street said the public was suffer-

ing from an epidemic of speculative insanity;
that Colonel Treadwell was merely a bold operator "backed" by a clique of the greatest fortunes
in America; that he was not a skilful "manipulator" of values, but by sheer brute force of tre-
mendous buying he made those stocks advance
with which he was identified and that, of course,
the public always follows the stocks that are made
active; and many other explanations. But in
the end Wall Street came to realize exactly to
what it was that the blind devotion of the speculative public for the colonel was due. Defying
all traditions, upsetting all precedents, violating
all rules, driving all the "veterans" to the verge
of hysterics and bankruptcy by his daily defiance
of accepted views as to the art of operating in
stocks, Colonel Josiah T. Treadwell founded a
new school: He told the truth.

The colonel sat in his office alone with his
thoughts. The door was open — it was always
open — and the clerks and customers of Treadwell & Co. as they passed to and fro caught
glimpses of the great leader's broad, kindly face
and shrewd, little, twinkling eyes that seemed to
smile at them. They wondered what new "deal"
the colonel was planning. And then they wished
with all their souls and purses they knew the name

of the stock — merely the name of it — so that
they might " get in on the ground floor."

The famous operator sat on a revolving chair
by his desk.   He had turned his back on an ac-
cumulation of correspondence and he now rotated
from right to left and from left to right.   The
tips of his shoes — he was a short man — missed
the floor by an inch or two and he swung his feet
contentedly.   A ticker whirred away blithely and
from time to time Treadwell ceased his rocking
and his foot-swinging, and glanced jovially at the
ticker " tape."   From his window he could see a
Mississippi of people or a bit of New York summer sky, but his restless eyes were roaming and
skipping from place to place.   And the clerks
and the customers wondered whether the market
was going the way the colonel had planned.   The
ticker was whirring and clicking, impassively, and
the colonel wore a meditative look.   What was the
" old man " scheming ?   The bears had better be
on their guard !   As a matter of fact, Josiah T.
Treadwell was thinking that his brother Wilson,
who had left him a few minutes before, was certainly growing bald.   He also wondered whether
people who advertised " restorers " and " invigo-
rators " were veracious or merely " Wall Streety "
as he put it to himself.

A young man, an utter stranger to Colonel Treadwell, halted at the door, and looked at the leader of the stock market, hesitatingly.

"Come in, come in," called out the colonel, cheerily. "Won't you walk into my parlor?"

"Good-morning, Colonel Treadwell," said the lad, diffidently.

"Who are you, and what are you, and what can I do for you?" said the colonel, extending his hand.

The youth did not heed the chubby, out-stretched hand. "My name," he said, very formally and introductorily, "is Carey. My father used to know you when he was editor of the *Blankburg Herald.*"

"Well," said the colonel, encouragingly, "shake hands anyhow."

Carey shook hands; his diffidence vanished. He was a pleasant-faced, pleasant-voiced young fellow, Treadwell thought. He was a good-hearted, jocular old fellow, unlike what he had imagined the leader of the stock market would be, Carey thought.

"Yes," went on the colonel, "I remember your father very well. I never forget my up-the-State friends, and I am always glad to see their sons. When I ran for Congress, Bill Carey wrote

red-hot editorials in my favor, and I was beaten
by a large and enthusiastic majority.   I haven't
seen your father in twenty-odd years — not since
he went wrong and took to politics."

"Well, Colonel Treadwell," laughed Carey, "I
guess Dad did his best for you. And if you didn't
go to Congress you're better off, from all I have
read in the papers about you."

You would have thought they had known each
other for years.

"That's what I say ; I have to," chuckling.

"Colonel," said the young man, boldly, "I've
come to ask your advice."

"Most people don't ask it twice.   Be careful
now."

"Do you mean that they get so rich following
it that they don't have to come again?"

"You are a politician, young man.   You'll
wake up and find yourself in Congress, some fine
day, unless your father goes back to newspaper
work and writes some editorials in *your* favor."

The boy had a pleasant smile, the colonel
thought.

"I have saved up some money, Colonel."

"Keep it.   That's the best advice I can give
you.   Go away instantly.   Great Scott, young-
ster, you are in Wall Street now."

"Oh, I — I'm safe enough in this office, I guess," retorted Carey.

The famous leader of the stock market looked at him solemnly. The boy returned the look, imperturbably. Then Colonel Treadwell laughed, and Carey laughed back at him.

"What are you doing to keep out of State's prison?" asked Treadwell.

"I'm a clerk in the office of the Federal Pump Company, third floor, upstairs. I have saved some money and I want to know what to do with it. I read an article in the *Sun* the other day. It said you had advised people to put their savings into Suburban Trolley and how well they had fared."

"That was a year ago. Trolley has gone up 50 points since then."

"That shows how good the advice was. And you also said a young man should do something with his savings and not let them lie idle." The young man looked straight into the little, twinkling, kindly eyes of the leader of the stock market.

"How much money have you?"

"I have two hundred and ten dollars," replied the lad with an uncertain smile. He had felt proud of the magnitude of his savings in his own room ; in this office he felt a bit ashamed of their insignificance.

"Dear me," said the millionaire speculator, very seriously, "that is a good deal of money. It's a blame sight more'n I had, when I started in business. Got it with you?"

"Yes, sir."

"Well, I'll introduce you to my brother Wilson, who has charge of our customers. Come in, John."

"John" came in. His other name was Mellen. He was a slim, quiet-looking man of about five-and-fifty. His enemies said that he had made $1,000,000 for every year he had lived and had kept it.

"Sit down, John," said Colonel Treadwell, shaking hands with Mr. Mellen, "I'll be back in a minute."

At the door he shook hands with two more visitors — a tall, ruddy-faced, white-haired, and white-whiskered man, Mr. Milton Steers, after-dinner speaker and self-confessed wit; and, incidentally, president of a railroad system; also Mr. D. M. Ogden, who looked like an English clergyman and was the owner of the huge Ogden Buildings in Wall Street. They had come to discuss the advisability of a new deal in "Trolley." They represented, they and their associates, more than $500,000,000. But Colonel Treadwell made them wait while he escorted his new acquaintance to his brother's room.

"Wilse," he said, "I've brought you a new customer, Mr. Carey."

Wilson P. Treadwell smiled pleasantly. He was a tall, slender man with a serious look. The firm did not desire new accounts, for there was already more business than could be handled. They were the busiest and the best-known stock brokers in the United States. But the colonel's friends were welcome, always.

"I'm very glad to meet Mr. Carey," said Wilson Treadwell. The firm had some very youthful customers; but their means were in inverse ratio to their years.

"I think," said the colonel, "that we had better buy some Easton & Allentown for him." He was smiling; he generally did. Moreover, he was thinking of his brother's mistaken impression of the new customer.

"That is a good idea," assented Wilson. "You ought to put in your order at once. The stock is going up very fast, Mr. Carey."

"Well, young man, give him your margin and let him buy you as much as he thinks best," said the colonel.

"Five thousand shares?" suggested Wilson Treadwell.

Colonel Treadwell chuckled. "Five thousand? A paltry five?"

"Well, fifty thousand if he wants them, and you guarantee his account," said his brother with a smile.

"I guess," said the leader of the stock market, slowly, "that you had better begin with one hundred shares."

Then Wilson, who knew his brother thoroughly, said "Oh!" and smiled and gave an order to a clerk to buy one hundred shares of Easton & Allentown Railroad stock at the "market" or prevailing price, for Mr. Carey, and took the boy's two hundred and ten dollars with the utmost gravity. The smallest Stock Exchange house would not accept such a pitiful account. Treadwell & Co. being the largest, would and did.

The colonel shook hands with young Carey, whose father had once edited a country newspaper, but who had never been an intimate friend, told him to "Come again, any time," and went back to his accomplices.

Easton & Allentown stock was the "feature" of the market that week and the next. Ten days after Carey had bought his hundred shares at 94 the stock sold at 106.

The young man went into the office of Tread-well & Co., on the eleventh day. He knew he had made a great deal of money — more than he had ever thought of having at his age — but he did not know what to do now. He heard one man say to another: "Take profits? Not at this price. E. & A. is sure to go to 115."

Carey figured that if he waited for the stock to sell at 115, he would make nearly a thousand dollars more.

"There is no use of being a blamed hog," the man continued, with picturesque emphasis, "but where in blazes is the sense of throwing away that much money by selling out too soon? Limit your losses and let your profits run."

They stood in the corridor of the partitioned office, the crowd of men, all of them customers of Treadwell & Co., excepting the newspaper report-ers who had called for their usual daily interview with the famous leader of the stock market. There were two United States Senators; an ex-Congressman; a score of men who had inherited fortunes and were doubling them in the stock market; three or four gray-haired shrewd-faced capitalists whose names appeared many times in the financial pages of newspapers; a baker's dozen of prominent municipal politicians, a well-known Western railroad president with a ruddy face and a snow-white beard; two famous physicians; the vice-president of a life insurance company; a half score of wholesale merchants and a low-voiced, insignificant little man, with a quiet, almost apologetic look, who seldom spoke and never smiled, but who, next to the colonel himself, was beyond question the heaviest "plunger" in the office.

The colonel came out of his office to go to his brother's room, where, seated about a long polished table were several directors of the Suburban Trolley Company — men to whom the newspapers always referred not by name but as "prominent insiders." It was a very important gathering. It involved no less than a final understanding in regards to the great "Trolley pool" whose operations, later on, were to become historical in Wall Street. It was, as one of the speculators outside put it, "a case of show down" — the cash resources available for pool purposes were to be ascertained, each man announcing the proportion of the 100,000 shares for which he was willing to "put up."

Carey was standing by the door of Wilson

Treadwell's office.   He did not feel altogether
comfortable, among so many elderly and obviously
very rich men.   His diffidence was the saving of
him for as the colonel passed he paused and said,
in a low voice : " Got your stock yet ? "

The customers in the corridor, men who, by the
colonel's advice, were " carrying " from 500 to
10,000 shares each of Easton & Allentown, leaned
forward eagerly.   All were men who north of
Wall Street would not have stooped to listen to
others' conversations if their lives depended on it.
In a broker's office, when the leader of the stock
market was speaking, such notions were absurd,
almost wicked.   Certainly, at that moment,
twenty pairs of eyes were looking fixedly at the
great leader of the stock market and the young
clerk.

The colonel felt this intuitively.   He confirmed
it with a quick glance of his sharp little eyes.
He had not sold all his Easton & Allentown, but
was disposing of it just as fast as the market
would take it.   It was not likely that the stock
would go much higher.   Wall Street, ever loath
to believe well of any stock operator, used to
comment sneeringly on the fact that the world
heard much about the " Treadwell buying " but
never a word about the Treadwell selling.

If the colonel gave a hint to the customers there would be an avalanche of selling orders that would make the price of the stock break sharply, and this would not benefit anyone.   He had advised them to buy the stock at 90 and at 95 — it was 105 now.   He had more than done his duty. If they did not sell out, in the hope of making more, it was their own lookout.

But there was the boy with the one hundred shares, the pleasant little clerk from up-the-State, who had brought in his entire fortune, his accumulated savings of two hundred and ten dollars. He was a stranger to Wall Street.   But supposing he should tell that he had been advised to sell ?   There would be the deuce to pay !

The colonel took chances.   Out of one corner of his mouth, so that he did not even turn his head toward the boy and so that the watching customers could not suspect what he was doing, he shot a quick whisper — a lob-sided but philanthropic affair — at him : " Look at the color of your money, boy !   Take your profits and say nothing ! "   And he walked into the room where the Suburban Trolley magnates awaited him impatiently.

Carey, thrilled but taciturn, gave his order to sell his Easton & Allentown, unsuspected by the mob. They sold it for him at 105⅛. Deducting commissions and interest charges the colonel's whisper had put $1,050 in the young clerk's pocket.

And the stock went a little higher and then declined slowly to about 99. The customers all made a great deal of money as it was, but not as much as they would have "taken out" of the Easton & Allentown "deal" if they had overheard that one of Colonel Treadwell's many whispers — lob-sided but philanthropic affairs!

THE MAN WHO WON

THE MAN WHO WON

" BROWN," said Mr. John P. Greener, as he turned
away from the ticker in the corner, " I wish you
would go over to the Board and see how the market is for Iowa Midland. Find out how much
stock there is for sale and who has it. It ought
to be pretty well distributed about the Street."

" What's up in it?" asked his partner, curiously.

" Nothing — yet," answered Greener, quietly.

He sat down at his desk and took up a letter,
headed " President's Office, Keokuk & Northern
Railway Company, Keokuk, Iowa." When he
had finished the entire sixteen closely written
pages, he arose and paced slowly up and down his
office.

He was a sallow-faced, black-bearded little
man, slender — almost frail looking — with a high
but rather narrow forehead. His eyes were furtive, shifty bits of brown light. He was thinking, and thinking to some purpose. Any one,
even a stranger, seeing him, would have known
that he was thinking of something big — the forehead was responsible for the impression ; and

131

also of something tricky, unscrupulous, cold-blood-
ed — his eyes were to blame there.   At length his
brow cleared. He muttered: "I must have
that road. Then, a consolidation with my Keokuk
& Northern ; and a new system that will endure
as long as the country !"

Brown returned in a half hour and reported.
There was very little stock for sale below $42 a
share — a few small lots held by unimportant commission houses.   The vendible supply increased at
44, and at 46 "inside stock would come out,"
which, translated into plain English, meant that
whenever the price of Iowa Midland Railway
Company stock rose to $46 per share, directors of
the company or close friends of theirs would be
found willing to part with their holdings.   It was
thus evident that the greater part of such stock
of the Iowa Midland as the Street was "carrying"
speculatively was not for sale at such a price as
would be regarded in the light of a great bargain
by Mr. John F. Greener, president *de facto* of the
rival Keokuk & Northern Railway, but better
known to countless "lambs" and widows and orphans and brother financiers as the Napoleon of
the Street.

"Any supporting orders?" piped Greener.
Stocks are "supported," or bought on declines,

so that the price shall not go down too much, and
above all not too quickly.

"Bagley has orders to buy 300 shares every
quarter of a point down until 37 is reached, and
then to take 5,000 shares at that figure.   He got
them direct from Willetts himself."   Bagley was
a broker who made a specialty of dealing in Iowa
Midland.   Willetts was the president of the company.

"Willetts," squeaked Greener, "was in Council
Bluffs this morning.   He is to take part in the
ceremonies of unveiling the Soldiers' Monument,
which begin at one o'clock — that is, within twenty
minutes, allowing for difference in time.   He will
be out of the reach of the telegraph for the afternoon."

Brown laughed.   "No wonder they are afraid
of you."

"Brown," said Greener, "start the movement
by selling 10,000 shares of Iowa Midland.   Divide
it up among the boys on the floor.   It would be
well if the room were frightened by the selling.
It is more important for us to get the price down
than to put out shorts at high figures.   I want
that stock down."   If he had merely desired to sell
the stock "short" he would have gone about it
carefully, to disturb the price as little as possible.

"If you want that I think you'll get it," said Brown. As he was going out Mr. Greener squeaked after him: "Keep them guessing, Brown; keep them guessing."

"That," mused Mr. John F. Greener, "ought to mean a three- or four-point break in Iowa Midland at the very least, and perhaps we can work through the peg at 37. We'll see." By the "peg" he meant the figure at which the supporting orders to buy were heaviest.

A few minutes later the Iowa Midland "post" on the floor of the Stock Exchange was surrounded by a dozen puzzled and apprehensive but gentlemanly brokers. And still a few minutes later the same spot was a seething whirlpool of maniacal humanity. It was appalling, the sight of these gesticulating, yelling, fighting, coat-tearing, fisticuffing brokers — appalling and vulgar, selfish, unpleasant, ungentlemanly but eminently typical. And all that caused the transformation was the fact that Mr. Brown had been seen whispering to Harry Wilson, and Harry Wilson had left him, gone to the Iowa Midland crowd, and sold 1,000 shares at $42\frac{1}{8}$ and 42. Then Mr. Brown had been seen speaking with W. G. Carleton in what struck witnesses as being a more or less agitated manner, and later Carleton had saun-

tered carelessly over to the Iowa Midland pre-
cinct, and, after displaying very great indifference
about the world in general, but most particularly
about the market for Iowa Midland, had sold
1,500 shares to Bagley, the specialist, at 41¾, 41⅝,
and 41½.   Mr. Brown was now watched by two or
three scores of sharp eyes, all having the same expression. And he was observed to look about
him apprehensively and then begin to converse
with Frank J. Pratt; whereupon Pratt, as fast as
his fat legs would carry him, hastened to "Iowa
Midland" and sold 2,000 shares at an average
price of 41.   The observant eyes had by this
taken on a new expression — of indecision; but
when they beheld Mr. Brown anxiously beckon to
his "particular" friend, Dan Simpson, and saw
shrill-voiced Dan rush like mad into the increasing crowd and sell 5,000 shares of Iowa Midland,
apparently regardless of price, the observant eyes
ceased to observe Brown. Activity was transferred
to their owners' throats as they thought to emulate Simpson and the rest of the Brown "whisperees."   Everybody scented danger, especially
as the same "whisperees" had not "given up"
the name of Brown & Greener as the real sellers,
but had sold as though each Brown-talked man
was acting for himself — which every other man in

the room knew was out of the question, and which,
in turn, increased the general uneasiness. It was
a confident and yet a mystifying movement. It
became more maddeningly perplexing when certain brokers, believed to be " close to the inside,"
also began to sell the stock. Everybody started
to do likewise. And everybody asked the same
question — " What's the matter? " — and received
an avalanche of answers, all different but all un-
favorable. One man said it was crop failures,
another mentioned divers kinds of bugs, a third
asserted it was extensive wash-outs and ruinous
landslides, and bankrupting attacks by a socialistic
legislature, and receivership probabilities.

Each of these was a good and sufficient reason
why Iowa Midland stock should be sold. The
comparison is odiously trite, but the growth of an
adverse rumor in Wall Street really resembles nothing so much as the traditional snowball rolling
down a hillside and becoming larger and larger as
it rolls, until it is huge, terrific, with appalling
possibilities for evil.

The Board Room became Iowa-Midland-mad.
Speculators often stampede — just like other an-
imals. No stock can withstand their rush to sell,
even though it be " protected " or " supported "
by its manipulators, much less a stock like Iowa

Midland, whose market sponsor was out of town, and out of reach of the telegraph.

From all over the room men rushed to Brown, who was sitting calmly at the Erie "post," chatting pleasantly with a friend.

"Brown, what's up in Iowa Midland?" one of them asked, feverishly. The others listened eagerly.

Brown might have said, "I don't know," rudely, and turned his back on them. But he did not. He responded jocularly: "It seems to me that something is down in Iowa Midland, that something being about three points, I should say. Ha! ha!"

By this time nearly all the listeners had concluded that, since Brown refused to tell, there must be something serious —— something very serious. Brown obviously was still selling the stock through other brokers, and would keep the bad news to himself until he had marketed his "line." After that, probably he would become interestingly garrulous. They therefore advised their respective offices to get rid of their Iowa Midland stock. It might be all right; but it might be all wrong. And it was going down fast.

Mr. Greener in his office was looking at the "tape" as it came out of the little electrical printing machine that records the transactions and prices.

The sallow-faced little man permitted himself a slight — a very slight — smile. The tape showed: "IA. MID., 1000. 39 ; 300. 38$\frac{3}{4}$; 500. $\frac{5}{8}$; 300. $\frac{1}{2}$; 200. $\frac{3}{8}$; $\frac{1}{4}$; 300. 38."

He turned away to summon a clerk, to whom he said : " Mr. Rock, please send for Mr. Coolidge. Make haste."

" Very well, sir."

A portly, white-waistcoated, white-haired man, with snow-white, short-cropped side whiskers, burst unceremoniously into the room.

" How do you do, Mr. Ormiston ? " squeaked Greener, cordially.

" Greener," panted the portly man, " what's the matter with Iowa Midland ? "

" How should I know ? " in a half-complaining, half-petulant squeak.

" Brown started the selling. I saw it myself. Greener, I did you a good turn once in Central District Telegraph. I'm long 6,000 shares of this Iowa Midland. For God's sake, man, if you know anything —— "

" Mr. Ormiston, all I know is what I learn from my confidential reports of the Iowa crop. Along the line of the Keokuk & Northern the crop is not what I hoped for." And he shook his head dolefully.

" *Ticky - ticky - ticky tick!* " said the ticker, calmly.

The portly man approached the little machine. " Thirty-seven-and-an-eighth. Thirty-seven ! " he shouted. " Great Scott ! she's going down like a ——— " He did not finish the comparison, but rushed out of the office without pausing to say good-by. At one o'clock his 6,000 shares at $42½ represented $255,000. Now, at two o'clock, at $37, the same stock would fetch about $222,000. A depreciation of $33,000 in an hour is apt to make one neglectful of the little niceties. An additional un-nicety was the obvious fact that an attempt to sell 6,000 shares on a declining market would inevitably cause a still further drop. Mr. Ormiston was excusable.

Again Mr. Greener summoned a confidential clerk.

" Mr. Rock," he squeaked, placidly, " telephone Mr. Brown that Ormiston, Monkhouse & Co. are about to sell 6,000 shares of Iowa Midland, and that Mr. Coolidge must not pay more than 35 for it.

" Mr. Coolidge is in your private room, sir," announced an office-boy.

The little financier, with an expressionless, sallow face, confronted his chief confidential broker. Their relations were unsuspected by the Street. Everybody thought Coolidge was a pleasant and honorable man.

"Coolidge, go to the Board at once. Ormiston is going to sell 6,000 shares of Iowa Midland. Get it as cheap as you can. Don't be in a hurry, though."

"How much shall I buy?" asked the broker, jotting down a few figures in his order book.

"As much as you can; all that is offered below 37," squeaked the Napoleon of the Street. It was a Napoleonic order. "And, Coolidge, I don't want this known by any one. Clear the stock yourself." It meant that Mr. Coolidge was to put the stock through the Clearing House in his own name. As there is a charge for this service, in addition to the usual buying or selling commission, such steps are not resorted to unless it is desired to conceal the identity of the broker's principal, should the latter be a fellow-member of the Exchange.

"Very well, Mr. Greener. Good-morning." And the broker went out on a run. "Whew!" he whistled when he was in the Street on his way to the Stock Exchange, a few doors below. "Brown

& Greener must be short at least **50,000** or **60,-
000 shares."** This was five times too much. But
it showed that Mr. Greener was impartial in his
distribution of erroneous impressions. He wanted
to accumulate the stock rather than " cover " a
short line ; but there was no reason why even his
most trusted broker should know it.

Ormiston's **6,000** shares found their way to **Mr.**
Coolidge's office at from **34⅞** to **35¾**. Mr. Brown
in the meantime had succeeded in forcing down
the prices by the usual tricks. The man who
once had done Greener a good turn now did him
another — the gift of **$40,000** !

In addition, Coolidge, employing several brokers,
purchased **23,000** shares in all, which meant that
Mr. Greener, after "covering" Brown's early
" short sales," was in possession of fully **14,000**
shares of the common stock of the **Iowa Midland**
Railway Company, at a price averaging nearly **6**
points lower than they could have been bought
on the preceding day, which is to say **$75,000**
cheaper.

But Brown & Greener had made as much on
their short sales, which was actually equivalent to
having the lambs pay a man for the privilege of
being shorn by him !

Such was the first of a series of skirmishes by

means of which the diminutive Napoleon of the Street captured the floating supply of Iowa Midland stock, until he had no less than 65,000 shares safe in his clutches.

All the old tricks that he knew and new devices he invented were used to hide from the Street the fact that Mr. Greener was buying the stock on every opportunity. But beyond a certain limit extensive purchases of a particular stock cannot be concealed from the thousand shrewd men who make their living — a very good living, indeed — by not being blind. First one thing, then another, told these men that some powerful financier or group of financiers had bought enormously of Iowa Midland, "absorbing" unostentatiously all the stock shaken out by the violent fluctuations of the past few months. This fact and the remarkable improvement of business along the line of the road caused a "substantial rise" in the price of the company's securities. But no one suspected the little Napoleon with the shifty eyes and the squeak and the genius, who had bought in the open market, through unsuspected brokers, and in Iowa from the local holders, by means of secret agents, until he had accumulated 78,600 shares.

Brown said to his partner one day, a little uneasily : "Supposing we can't get any more stock,

what are we going to do with what we have?"
To try to sell it, however carefully, would be sure
to break the market.

"Brown," squeaked the little man, plaintively,
"I have concluded that in case I can't get enough
stock to bring Willetts and his crowd"—the
president of the Iowa Midland and his fellow-
directors—"to my way of thinking, we had better sell the block we now hold to the Keokuk &
Northern Railway Company at the market price
of $68 a share. Perhaps we could even run it up
a little higher. Our stock cost us on an average
$51 a share. We could take our payment one
half in cash and half in first mortgage bonds at a
fair discount. The deal would be highly bene-
ficial to the Keokuk & Northern Company, since,
having such a large block of her rival's stock,
there would be no more fighting and rate-cutting.
Our company would be a powerful factor in the
Iowa Midland's affairs, for we ought to have two
or possibly three directors in their board."

"Greener," said Brown, "shake!"

"Oh, no; not yet," squeaked the little man,
deprecatingly.

Shortly afterward began a campaign of hostility against the management of the Iowa Midland
Railway Company and President Willetts in par-

ticular.   It was a bitter campaign of defamation,
of ingenious accusations, and of alarming prog-
nostications.   All the newspapers, important or
obscure, subsidized or honest, began to print
articles of the kind technically known as "roasts."
The road, it was declared, had escaped a receivership by a sheer miracle.   President Willetts's in-
competence was stupendous and incurable.   There
was, in sooth, some basis for the complaints, and
many stockholders were undoubtedly dissatisfied
with the Willetts "dynasty."   But not even the
newspapers themselves knew that they were merely
moving in response to wires artistically pulled by
a financial genius of the first water.   The stock
once more declined.   Not knowing who was fighting him, President Willetts was unable to defend
himself effectively.   Many timid or disgusted
holders sold out.   Mr. Greener gave no sign of
life ; but his brokers bought the stock offered for
sale.

At length a well-known and talkative broker
confided to an intimate friend, who told his intimate friend in confidence, who whispered to his
chum, who told, etc., etc., that Mr. John F.
Greener had been responsible for the fall and
rise of Iowa Midland stock ; that for months he
had been buying it on the Stock Exchange ; that

he had quietly picked up some large blocks in
Iowa. All of which was very sad, and, worse still,
true. Also, that Mr. Greener now held 182,300
shares of the stock, which was even sadder, but
untrue.

It really was very well done. The annual meeting of the company was only six weeks away.

The reporters rushed to Mr. Greener's office.
The little financier would not be seen. At length
he reluctantly consented to be interviewed. He
admitted, after a skilful display of unwillingness,
that he had bought Iowa Midland stock. As to
the amount, he said that was not of interest to
the general public. The reporters finally cornered him and succeeded in making the little
financier say, with a fleeting and very peculiar
smile: "Yes; it *is* over 100,000 shares." And
not another word could the newspaper men get
out of him.

Being an intelligent man, he never lied for
publication. Each reporter who saw that smile
and the furtive look that accompanied it went
away convinced to the life-wagering point that
Mr. John F. Greener was in control of the Iowa
Midland. And they wrote accordingly.

President Willetts all but had an apoplectic
stroke. The Street disgustedly said: " Another

successful, villainous plot of Greener's!" And such was his reputation as an "absorber" of roads and roads' profits that the stock declined ten points in two days. Investors and speculators alike displayed a frantic desire not to be identified in any way or manner with one of Mr. Greener's properties.

The little financier had not been mistaken. His last card was his own evil reputation! He had reserved it for the end. On the wide-spread fear that followed his broker's artistic "indiscretion" he was able to "scoop" 32,000 shares more at low figures. Such is the value of fame!

He now held 110,600 shares, or one third of the Iowa Midland Railroad Company's entire capital stock — enough to coerce Willetts into making very profitable arrangements with Mr. Greener's Keokuk & Northern Railway Company. Of course the absolute control of the Iowa Midland was best of all, if it only could be secured. But of this the sallow-faced little man with the high forehead and the shifty eyes was doubtful. He confessed as much to Brown, ending with : "It's a shame, too. I could make so much out of that property!"

He estimated — it had cost him $11,000 to secure the necessary data — that Willetts and his

clique held 105,000 shares, so that there were
still 122,000 shares unaccounted for — probably
scattered among small investors throughout the
country, who did not care who managed the road
so long as they received pleasant promises of
dividends, and also among banking houses and
anti-Greener men, who, though they did not
approve of Willetts, disapproved even more
emphatically and vehemently of Greener and his
methods.

If he could not buy the stock itself he must
try to secure proxies.

He knew that some of the trust companies held
a fair amount of the longed-for stock. He laid
siege to them. He bombarded them with promises and poured an enfilading fire of pledges so
honorable, so eminently sound and business-like,
as to pierce the armor of their distrust. In the
end they actually grew to believe that they were
acting wisely when they pledged their support
to Mr. Greener. The guarantee he gave them
seemed ironclad, and they agreed to give him their
proxies whenever he should send for them.

He called his clerk Rock and told him: "Go
to the Rural Trust Company and to the Commercial Loan & Trust Company. See Mr. Rob-
erts and Mr. Morgan. They will give you some

Iowa Midland proxies made out to Frederick Rock or John F. Greener."

Rock was a good-looking, quiet chap, with a very well-shaped head and a resolute chin. His manners were pleasing. He had a habit of looking one straight in the eyes, but did not always succeed thereby in conveying an impression of straightforwardness. But he certainly impressed one as being bold and keen. His fellow-clerks used to say that Rock spent his spare time in studying the financial operations of the Napoleon of the Street with the same care and minuteness that military students go over the campaigns of Napoleon Bonaparte — which was the truth.

"Mr. Greener," said Rock, "you are carrying 110,000 shares of stock, are you not?"

"Eh?" squeaked Greener, innocently.

"I figure that, unless you are doing something outside this office, you will need proxies for 50,-000 shares more to give you absolute control and elect your own board of directors and carry out your plans in connection with Keokuk & Northern."

Not by so much as the twinkling of an eye did the little man betray that he was interested in Rock's words, or that the clerk's meddling with the firm's affairs was at all out of the ordinary.

"Mr. Greener," said the clerk, very earnestly, "I should like to try to get them for you."

"Yes?" he squeaked, absent-mindedly.

"Yes, sir," answered Rock.

"Go ahead, then," said Mr. Greener, carelessly. "Let me know next week how you are getting on."

An expression of disappointment came into Rock's face, whereupon Greener added: "Of course if you succeed I'll do well by you."

"What will you do, Mr. Greener?" asked the clerk, looking straight at him.

"I'll give you," he squeaked, encouragingly, "ten thousand dollars."

"Is that a good price for the work, Mr. Greener? I may have to pay out a great deal," added the young clerk with a faint touch of bitterness.

"It is all that it is worth to me, Mr. Rock, and I think it is worth more to me than to anybody else. I'll raise your salary from sixteen hundred to two thousand a year. That's a great deal more money than I had at your age, Mr. Rock.

"Very well," said Rock, quietly. "I'll do the best I can." But once away from Greener, his face flushed with anger and indignation. "Ten thousand for what might be worth ten millions to the financier!" The clerk had studied Greener's

Napoleonic methods for two years. He had learned patience for one thing, and he had waited for his chance. It had come at last, and he knew it.

Events make the man. Rock had thought carefully, intelligently, and, best of all, coolly. He had planned logically. It was a good plan; it was the only feasible plan, and it could not be upset by meddlesome courts. How Mr. John F. Greener had failed to think of the same plan was a bit strange. The unscrupulousness of it did not frighten the clerk. He had the instincts of a financier of the Greener school.

The clerk all that week did nothing but collect the Iowa Midland proxies promised by the complaisant trust companies. They amounted to 21,200 shares. From prominent brokerage houses, by means of alluring and unauthorized promises, he secured 7,100 shares; in all he had 28,300 shares. This meant that at the approaching annual meeting Mr. Greener could vote 138,900 shares out of a possible total of 320,000. Unless the opposition could unite, the election was already sure to " go Mr. Greener's way."

From time to time, when the little financier would ask Rock how he was progressing, the clerk would tell him he was doing as well as could be

expected. He also told Mr. Greener that the
trust companies had given only 14,000 shares,
and he said nothing whatever of the 7,100 shares
he had secured from the friendly brokers. It
was a desperate risk, this concealing from Mr.
Greener how well he had done; but the clerk
was bold.

The moment Rock became convinced that there
were no more pro-Greener proxies to be had by
hook or crook, he began his attack on the enemy.
His problem was to capture the anti-Greener votes
— or stock. He proceeded to put his plan into
effect. And the plan of this healthy clerk with
the unflinching eyes and the resolute chin was
worthy of the sallow-faced little man with the furtive look and the great forehead.

"It is a case of *heads I win; tails you lose*,"
Rock muttered to himself, exultingly.

The young man presented himself forthwith at
the office of Weddell, Hopkins & Co., prominent
bankers and bitter enemies of Mr. John F. Greener
and his methods. They knew Rock as one of the
confidential clerks of Brown & Greener, and he
had no difficulty in securing an audience from Mr.
Weddell.

"Good-morning, Mr. Weddell."

"Good-morning, sir," said the banker, coldly.

"I must say I'm somewhat surprised at the presumption of your people in sending you to me."

"Mr. Weddell," said Rock, a trifle too eagerly to be artistic, "I've left the firm of Brown & Greener. They were," he added, youthfully, "too rascally for me."

Mr. Weddell's face froze solid. He feared an application for a position.

"Ye—es?" he said. His voice matched his face in frigidity.

"Mr. Weddell," said the young clerk, looking straight into the old banker's eyes, "you in common with other honest men have been wishing you could prevent Mr. Greener from wrecking the Iowa Midland. Now, Mr. Weddell," he went on, eagerly, as the enthusiasm of the plan grew upon him, "I know all about Mr. Greener's plans and resources and I want you to help me fight him. If you do we will win, sure."

"How will you go about it?" asked the old banker, evasively. He was not certain this was not some trick of the versatile Mr. John F. Greener.

"Mr. Greener," answered young Rock, "has not control of the property. He has only 110,600 shares. I had access to the books, and I know to a share."

"I don't wish you to betray an employer's se-

crets, even though he may be my enemy.   I do
not care to hear any more." He was an old-
fashioned banker, was Mr. Weddell.

"I am not betraying any secrets. He himself
said he had over 100,000 shares, and all the reporters jumped at the conclusion that he had
actually a controlling interest. And that is what
he will have, unless you help me. I have proxies
here for 28,300 shares from trust companies and
commission houses. My plan is to get all the
proxies I can from the anti-Greener and the anti-
Willetts stockholders. Then we can make Mr.
Willetts give us pledges in black and white to in-
augurate the much-needed reforms and stop his
policy of extravagance and his costly traffic arrangements. Willetts will do it to save himself
and the road from falling into Greener's hands.
But there's no time to lose, Mr. Weddell." The
excitement of the game he was playing stimulated
him like wine.

"And you?" queried the old banker, meaningly. "Where do *you* come in?" The insinuation
was his last weapon. The young man's was really
the only feasible plan that he could see.

"I? It might be, Mr. Weddell, that after the
election I could be appointed assistant secretary
of the company, as an evidence of good faith on

the part of the reform management. I can keep tabs on them and represent the Weddell-Hopkins interest. The salary," he added, with truly artistic significance, "could be $5,000 a year. I have been getting just one-half that." His salary was exactly $1,600; but why minimize one's commercial value?

The old banker walked up and down. . . .

"By gad, sir, you shall have our proxies," said Mr. Weddell, at length.

"It would be well not to let Mr. Greener suspect this," added Rock. And the banker agreed with him.

Weddell, Hopkins & Co. held 14,000 shares of Iowa Midland stock, and on the next day Rock received their proxies. Coming from so well-known, so notoriously anti-Greener a house, they served as credentials to him, and he was able to convince many doubting Thomases. He secured proxies from practically all the anti-Greener stock held in the city, as well as in Philadelphia and Boston.

His day-long absences from the office aroused no suspicions there, since everybody thought he was working in the interest of Brown & Greener, including Messrs. Brown & Greener. All told, the proxies he had secured from Mr. Greener's

friends and from his foes amounted to 61,830
shares. It was really a remarkable performance.
He felt very proud of it. As to consequences, he
had carefully weighed them. He was working for
Frederick Rock. He was bound to succeed, on
whichever side the coin came down.

Mr. Greener called him into the private office.

" Mr. Rock, how about those Iowa Midland
proxies ? "

" I have them safe," answered the clerk, a bit
defiantly.

" How many ? "

Rock pulled out a piece of paper, though he
knew the figures by heart. He said, in a tone he
endeavored to make nonchalant : " I have exactly
61,830 shares."

" What ? What ? " The Napoleon's voice over-
flowed with astonishment.

Rock looked straight into Greener's shifty brown
eyes. " I said," he repeated, " that I had proxies
for 61,830 shares."

Mr. Greener remembered himself. " I congratulate you, Mr. Rock, on keeping your word. You
will find I keep mine equally well," he said in his
normal squeak.

" We may as well have an understanding now
as any other time, Mr. Greener." Rock's eyes did

not leave the sallow face of the great railroad
wrecker. He knew he had crossed the Rubicon.
He was fighting for his future, for the prosperity
of his dreams. And he was fighting a giant of
giants. All this the clerk thought; and the
thought braced him wonderfully. He became
self-possessed, discriminating — a Napoleonic bud
about to burst into full bloom.

"What do you mean?" squeaked Mr. Greener,
naïvely.

Mr. Brown entered. He was just in time to
hear the clerk say: "You have, all told, 110,000
shares of Iowa Midland. President Willetts and
his crowd control about the same amount."

"Yes," said the sallow-faced little man. His
forehead was moist — barely moist — with perspi-
ration, but his face was expressionless. His eyes
were less furtive; that was all. He was looking
intently now at the young clerk, for he understood.

"Well, some of the proxies stand in the name
of Frederick Rock or John F. Greener, but the
greater part in my name alone. I can vote the
entire lot as I please. And whichever side I vote
for will have an absolute majority. Mr. Greener,
I have the naming of the directors, and therefore
of the president of the Iowa Midland. And you

can't prevent me ; and you can't touch me ; and
you can't do a d—d thing to me ! " he ended, defiantly.   It was nearly all superfluous, inartistic.
But, youth — a defect one overcomes with time !

"You infernal scoundrel ! " shouted Mr. Brown.
He had a short, thick neck, and anger made his
face dangerously purple.

"I secured most of the proxies," continued
Rock, in a tone that savored slightly of self-defence,
"by assuring Weddell, Hopkins & Co. and their
friends that I would vote against Mr. Greener."
He paused.

"Go ahead, Mr. Rock," squeaked Mr. Greener ;
"don't be afraid to talk."   The pale little man
with the black beard and the high forehead not
only had a great genius for finance, but possessed
wonderful nerve.   His squeak was an inconsist-
ency ; but it served to make him human.

"You offered me $10,000 cash and $2,000 a
year."

"Yes," admitted Mr. Greener, meekly.   "How
much do you want ? "   His look became furtive
again.   A great weight had been removed from
his mind.   Rock perceived it and became even
more courageous.

"Weddell, Hopkins & Co. and their friends
want me to vote the Willetts ticket, Mr. Willetts

having promised to make important reforms. My
reward is to be the position of assistant secretary,
with headquarters in New York, at a salary of
$5,000 a year, to say nothing of the backing of
Weddell, Hopkins & Co."

" I'll do as much and give you $20,000 in cash,"
said Mr. Greener, quietly.

" No.   I want to join the New York Stock
Exchange.   I want you to buy me a seat and I
want you to give me some of your business.   And
I want you to lend me $50,000 on my note."

" Yes ? "

" Mr. Greener, you know what I can do ; and
I know what the absolute control of the Iowa Midland means to you, and what the consolidation with
Keokuk & Northern or the lease of the one by the
other would do for both of them — and for you.
And I want to be your broker.   I'll serve you
faithfully, Mr. Greener."

" Rock," squeaked Mr. Greener, " shake hands.
I understand just how you feel about this.   I'll
buy you a seat and I'll give you all the business I
can, and I'll lend you $100,000 without any note.
I think I know you now.   The seat you shall have
just as soon as it can be bought.   My interests
shall be your interests in the future."

" I've made all the necessary arrangements.   I

can buy the seat at a moment's notice," said Rock, calmly, though his heart was beating wildly for sheer joy of victory. "It will cost $23,000."

"Tell Mr. Simpson to make out my personal check for $25,000," piped the Napoleon of the Street, almost cordially.

"Th-thank you very much, Mr. Greener," stammered the bold clerk. "The proxies ———"

"Oh, that's all right," interrupted Mr. John F. Greener. "You'll go to Des Moines with us. You're one of us now. I've long wanted a man like you. But, Rock, nowadays, young men are either gamblers or fools," he added, with a final plaintive squeak.

A week later Mr. Greener was elected president of the Iowa Midland Railway Company and Mr. Rock was elected a member of the New York Stock Exchange.

THE LOST OPPORTUNITY

THE LOST OPPORTUNITY

For many years Daniel Dittenhoeffer had desired the ruin of John F. Greener. "Dutch Dan," as the Street called Dittenhoeffer was a burly man with very blonde hair, a very red nose and a very loud voice. Greener was a sallow, swarthy bit of a man, with black hair and a squeaky voice. He had furtive brown eyes and a very high forehead; while Dittenhoeffer had frank blue eyes and the pugnacious chin and thick neck of a prize fighter. Both were members of the New York Stock Exchange but Greener was never seen on the "floor" after one of his victims lifted him bodily by the collar and dropped him fifteen feet into a coal cellar on Exchange Place. He would plan the wrecks of railroad systems as a measure preliminary to their absorption, just as a boa constrictor crushes its victims into pulp the more easily to swallow them. But the practice, unchecked for years, had made him nervous and soul-fidgetty.

Dan spent his days from 10 to 3 on the Stock Exchange and his nights from 10 to 3 at the roulette tables or before a faro lay-out. Restless as the quivering sea and suffering from chronic

insomnia, he had perforce to satisfy his constitu-
tional craving for powerful stimulants, but as he
hated delirium tremens he gave himself ceaselessly
big doses of the wine of gambling — it does as
much for the nerves as the very best whiskey. He
would buy or sell 50,000 shares of a stock and
he would bet $50,000 on the turn of a card. On
an occasion he offered to wager a fortune that he
could guess which of two flies that had alit on
a table would be the first to fly away. Greener
found, in the Stock Exchange, the means to a desired end. Despite innumerable bits of stock job-
bing, he had no exalted opinion, in his heart of
hearts, of stock operations. But Dittenhoeffer
thought the stock market was the court of last
resort, whither financiers should go, when they
were in the right, to get their deserts; and when
they were in the wrong to overcome their deserts by
the brute force of dollars. It was natural that in
their operations in the market the two men should
be as dissimilar as they were in their physical and
temperamental characteristics — Machiavelli and
Richard Cœur-de-Lion.

Nobody knew exactly how the enmity between
Greener and Dittenhoeffer began. The "Little
Napoleon of Railroading" had felt toward Dutch
Dan a certain passive hostility for interference

with sundry stock market deals.   But Dan hated
Greener madly, probably for the same reason that
a hawk may have for hating a snake : the instinc-
tive antipathy of the utterly dissimilar.

Scores of men had tried to " bust " Greener, but
Greener had grown the richer by their efforts, the
growth of his fortune being proportionate to the
contraction of theirs.   Sam Sharpe had come from
Arizona with $12,000,000 avowedly to show the
effete East how to crush " financial skunks of
the Greener class."   And the financial skunk
learned no new lesson, though the privilege of
imagining he was giving one cost Sharpe a half-
million a month for nearly one year.   Then, after
Sharpe had learned more of the game —— and of
Greener — he joined hands with Dittenhoeffer and
together they attacked Greener.   They were skilful stock operators, very rich and utterly without
financial fear.   And they loathed Greener.   In a
more gorgeous age they would have cut the Little
Napoleon to pieces and passed his roasted heart
on a platter around the festive board.   In the col-
orless XIX century they were fain to content
themselves with endeavoring to despoil him of his
tear-stained millions; to do which they united their
own smile-wreathed millions —— some seven or eight
of them —— and opened fire.   Their combined fortune

was divided into ten projectiles and one after another hurled at the little man with the squeaky
voice and the high forehead.   The little man
dodged the first and the second and the third, but
the fourth broke his leg and the fifth knocked the
wind out of him.   The Street cheered and showed
its confidence in the artillerists by going short of
the Greener stocks.   But just before the sixth
shot Greener called to his assistance old Wilbur
Wise, the man with the skin-flinty heart and
thirty millions in cash.   A protecting rampart,
man-high, of government bonds was raised about
the prostrate Napoleon and the financial cannon-
eers ceased firing precious projectiles.   The new
fortifications were impregnable and they knew it ;
so they contented themselves with gathering up
their own shot and a small railroad or two dropped
by Greener in his haste to seek shelter.   Then
Sharpe went to England to win the Derby and
Dittenhoeffer went to Long Branch to amuse himself playing a no-limit faro game that cost him
on an average $10,000 a night for a month.

There was a period of peace in Wall Street following the last encounter between the diminutive
Napoleon and Dutch Dan.   But after a few months
the fight resumed.   Greener was desirous of "bull-
ing" his stocks generally and his pet, Federal

Telegraph Company, particularly. Just to show there was no need to hurry the "bull" or upward movement Dan sold the stock "short" every time Greener tried to advance the price. Four times did Greener try and four times Dittenhoeffer sold him a few thousand shares — just enough to check the advance. Up to a certain point a manipulator of stocks is successful. His manipulation may comprise many ingenious and complex actions and devices, but the elemental fact in bull manipulation is to buy more than the other fellow can or wishes to sell. Greener was willing to buy, but Dan was even more willing to sell.

Greener really was in desperate straits. He was committed to many important enterprises. To carry them out he needed cash and the banks, fearful of stock market possibilities, were loath to lend him enough. Besides which, there was the desire on the part of the banks' directors to pick up fine bargains should their refusal to lend Greener money force him to throw overboard the greater part of his load. Greener had despoiled innumerable widows and orphans in his railroad wrecking schemes. The money lenders should avenge the widows and orphans. It was a good deed. There was not a doubt of it in their minds.

Federal Telegraph, in which Greener's commitments were heaviest, had been slowly sinking. Successful in other quarters of the market, Dutch Dan decided to "whack the everlasting daylights out of Fed. Tel." He went about it calmly, just as he played roulette — selling it methodically, ceaselessly, depressingly. And the price wilted. Greener, unsuccessful in other quarters of the Street, decided it was time to do something to save himself. He needed only $5,000,000. At a pinch $3,000,000 might do; or, for the moment, even $2,500,000. But he must have the money at once. Delay meant danger and danger meant Dittenhoeffer and Dittenhoeffer might mean death.

Of a sudden, rising from nowhere, fathered by no one, the rumor whirled about the Street that Greener was in difficulties. Financial ghouls ran to the banks and interviewed the presidents. They asked no questions in order to get no lies. They simply said, as though they knew: "Greener is on his uppers."

The bank presidents smiled, indulgently, almost pityingly: "Oh, you've just heard it, have you? We've known it for six weeks!"

Back to the Stock Exchange rushed the ghouls to sell the Greener stocks — not Federal Telegraph which was really a good property, but his reorganized roads, whose renascence was so recent that they had not grown into full strength. Down went prices and up went the whisper: "Dittenhoeffer's got Greener at last!"

A thousand brokers rushed to find their dear friend Dan to congratulate him — Napoleon's conqueror, the hero of the hour, the future dispenser of liberal commissions. But dear Dan could not be found. He was not on the "floor" of the Exchange nor at his office.

Some one had sought Dittenhoeffer before the brokers thought of congratulating him — some one who was the greatest gambler of all, greater even than Dutch Dan — a little man with furtive brown eyes and a squeaky voice; also a wonderful forehead: Mr. John F. Greener.

"Mr. Dittenhoeffer, I sent for you to ask you a question," he squeaked, calmly. He stood beside a garrulous ticker.

"Certainly, Mr. Greener." And Dittenhoeffer instantly had a vision of humble requests to "let up." And he almost formulated the very words of a withering refusal.

"Would you execute an order from me?"

"Certainly, Mr. Greener. I'll execute anybody's orders. I'm a broker."

"Very well. Sell 50,000 shares of Federal Telegraph Company for me."

"What price?" jotting down the figures, from force of habit, his mind being paralyzed.

"The best you can get. The stock," glancing at the tape, "is 91."

"Very well."

The two men looked at one another — Dutch Dan half menacingly, Greener, calmly, steadily, his furtive eyes almost truthful.

"Good-morning," said Dittenhoeffer at length and the little man's high-browed head nodded dismissingly.

Dittenhoeffer hastened back to the Exchange. At the entrance he met his partner, Smith — the "Co." of D. Dittenhoeffer & Co.

"Bill, I've just got an order from Greener to sell 50,000 shares of Federal Telegraph."

"Wh-what?" gasped Smith.

"Greener sent for me, asked me whether I'd accept an order from him, I said yes, and he told me to sell 50,000 shares of Telegraph, and I'm——"

"You've got him, Dan. You've got him," exultantly.

"I'm going to cover my 20,000 shares with the first half of the order and sell the rest the best I can."

"Man alive, this is your chance! Don't you
see you've got him? Smilie of the Eastern National Bank tells me there isn't a bank in the city
will lend Greener money, and he needs it badly to
pay the last $10,000,000 to the Indian Pacific
bondholders. He's bit off more than he can chew,
damn 'im!"

"Well, Bill, we'll treat Mr. Greener as we do
any other customer," said Dittenhoeffer.

"But——" began Smith, with undisguised consternation; he was an honest man, when away
from the Street.

"Oh, I'll get him yet. This won't save him.
I'll get him yet," with a confident smile.

It would have been very easy for him to take
advantage of Greener's order to make a fortune.
He was short 20,000 shares which he had put out
at an average price of 93. He could have taken
Greener's block of 50,000 shares and hurled it
bodily at the market. Not even a gilt-edge stock
could withstand the impact of such a fearful blow,
and the price of Federal Telegraph doubtless
would have broken 15 points or more, and he
could easily have taken in his shorts at 75 or possibly even at 70 —— which would have meant a
profit of a half-million of dollars —— and a loss of
a much needed million to his arch-foe, Greener.

And if he allowed his partner to whisper in strict confidence to some friend how Dan was selling out a big line of Telegraph for Greener the " Room " would have gone wild and everybody would have hastened to sell and the decline would have gone so much further as to cripple the little Napoleon possibly beyond all hope of recovery. Had Greener made the most colossal mistake of his life in giving the order to his enemy?

Dan went to the Federal Telegraph post where a score of madmen were shouting at the top of their voices the prices they were willing to pay or to accept for varying amounts of the stock. He gave to twenty brokers orders to sell 1,000 shares each at the best obtainable price and he himself, through another man took an equal amount. On the next day he in person sold 20,000 shares and on the third day the last 10,000 shares of Greener's order. This selling, the Street thought, was for his own account. It was all short stock; that is, his colleagues thought he was selling stock he didn't own, trusting later on to buy it back cheaply. Such selling never has the depressing effect of " long " stock because it is obvious that the short seller must sooner or later buy the stock in, insuring a future demand, which should exert a lifting influence on prices; for

" He who sells what isn't his'n
Must buy it back or go to pris'n."

And Dittenhoeffer was able to get an average of $86 per share for Greener's 50,000 shares of Federal Telegraph Company stock, for the Street agreed, with many headshakings, that Dan was becoming too reckless and Greener was a slippery little cuss and the short interest must be simply enormous and the danger of a bad " squeeze " exceedingly great.   Wherefore, they forebore to " whack " Telegraph.   Indeed, many shrewd traders saw, in the seeming weakness of the stock, a trap of the wily little Napoleon and they " fooled " him by astutely buying Federal Telegraph !

With the $4,300,000 which he received from the sale of the big block of stock, Greener overcame his other troubles and carried out all his plans. It was a daring stroke, to trust to a stock broker's professional honor.   It made him the owner of a great railroad system.   Dutch Dan's attacks later did absolutely no harm.   Greener had made an opportunity and Dittenhoeffer had lost one.

PIKE'S PEAK OR BUST

PIKE'S PEAK OR BUST

HE was only seventeen, fair-haired and rosy-cheeked, with girlish blue eyes, when he applied for the vacancy in the office of Tracy & Middleton, Bankers and Brokers. His name was Willis N. Hayward, and he was a proud boy, indeed, when he was selected out of twenty "applicants" to be telephone-clerk for the firm.

From 10 A.M. until 3 P.M. he stood by Tracy & Middleton's private telephone on the floor of the Stock Exchange — the Board Room — receiving messages from the office — chiefly orders to buy or sell stocks for customers — and transmitting the same messages to the "Board member" of the firm, Mr. Middleton; also telephoning Mr. Middleton's reports to the office. He spoke with a soft, refined voice, and his blue eyes beamed so ingenuously upon the other telephone-boys in the same row of booths, that they said they had a Sally in their alley, and they immediately nicknamed him Sally.

It was all very wonderful to young Hayward, who had been out of boarding-school but a few months — the excited rushing hither and thither

of worried-looking men, the frantic waving of
hands, the maniacal yelling of the brokers executing their orders about the various "posts," and
their sudden relapse into semi-sanity as they jot-
ted down the price at which they had sold or
bought stocks. It was not surprising that he
should fail to understand just how they did business ; but what most impressed him was the fact,
vouched for by his colleagues, that these same
clamoring, gesticulating brokers were actually
supposed to make a great deal of money. He
heard of "Sam" Sharpe's $100,000 winnings in
Suburban Trolley, and of "Parson" Black's famous
million-dollar *coup* in Western Delaware — the little gray man even being pointed out to him in
corroboration. But, then, he had also heard of
Aladdin and the Wonderful Lamp, and Jack the
Giant Killer.

He learned the business, as nearly all boys
must do in Wall Street, by absorption. If he
asked questions he received replies, but no one
volunteered any information for his guidance, and
in self-defence he was forced to observe closely, to
see how others did, and to remark what came of
it. He heard nothing but *speculate! speculate!*
in one guise or another, many words for the same
meaning. It was all buying or selling of stocks —

a concentrated and almost visible hope of making
much money in the twinkling of an eye.   Nobody
talked of anything else on the Exchange.   Bosom
friends met at the opening of business and did not
say "Good-morning," but plunged without pre-
amble into the only subject on earth — speculation.   And if one of them arrived late he inevitably inquired forthwith, "How's the market?"
— asked it eagerly, anxiously, as if fearful that
the market had taken advantage of his absence
to misconduct itself.   The air was almost un-
breathable for the innumerable "tips" to buy or
sell securities and insecurities of all kinds.   The
brokers, the customers, the clerks, the Exchange
door-keepers, all Wall Street read the morning
papers, not to ascertain the news, but to pick such
items as would, should, or might, have some effect
on stock values.   There was no god but the ticker,
and the brokers were its prophets!

All about Sally were hundreds of men who
looked as if they took their thoughts home with
them and dined with them and slept with them and
dreamed of them — the look had become settled, im-
mutable.   And it was not a pleasant look, about
the eyes and lips.   He saw everywhere the feverish-
ness of the "game."   Insensibly the atmosphere of
the place affected him, colored his thoughts, induced

certain fancies.   As he became more familiar with
the technique of the business he grew to believe,
like thousands of youthful or superficial observers,
that stock-market movements were comparable
only to the gyrations of the little ivory ball about
the roulette-wheel.   The innumerable tricks of
the trade, the uses of inside misinformation, the
rationale of stock-market manipulation, were a
sealed book to him.   He heard only that his
eighteen-year-old neighbor made $60 buying
twenty shares of Blue Belt Line on Thursday and
selling them on Saturday, $3\frac{3}{8}$ points higher; or
that Micky Welch, Stuart & Stern's telephone-boy,
had a "tip" from one of the big room traders which
he bravely "played" — as you "play" horse or
"play" the red or the black — and cleared $125 in
less than a week; or that Watson, a "two-dollar"
broker, made a "nice turn" selling Southern
Shore.   Or else he heard, punctuated with poignant oaths, how Charlie Miller, one of the New
Street door-keepers, lost $230 buying Pennsylva-
nia Central, after he accidentally overheard Archie
Chase, who was "Sam" Sharpe's principal broker,
tell a friend that the "Old Man" said "Pa.
Cent." was due for a ten-point rise; instead of
which there had been a seven-point decline.   Always the boy heard about the apparently irre-

sponsible " bulges " and " drops," of the winnings
of the men who happened to guess correctly, or
of the losses of those who had failed to " call the
turn." Even the vernacular of the place savored
of the technicalities of a gambling-house.

As time wore on the glamour of the game wore
off; likewise his scruples. His employers and their
customers — all gentlemanly, agreeable people —
speculated every day, and nobody found fault
with them. It was not a sin; it was a regular
business. And so, whenever there was a " good
thing," he " chipped in " one dollar to a telephone-
boys' " pool " that later operated in a New Street
bucket shop to the extent of ten shares. His
means were small, his salary being only $8 a
week; and very often he thought that if he only
had a little more money he would speculate on a
larger scale and profit proportionately. If each
time he had bought one share he had held twenty
instead, he figured that he would have made no
less than $400 in three months.

The time is ripe for other things when a boy
begins to reason that way. Having no scruples
against speculating, the problem with him became
not, " Is it wrong to speculate ? " but rather,
" What shall I do to raise money for margin purposes ? " It took nearly four months for him to

arrive at this stage of mind. With many boys the question is asked and satisfactorily solved within three weeks. But Hayward was an exceptionally nice chap.

Now, the position of telephone-boy is really important in that it requires not only a quick-witted but a trustworthy person to fill it. In the first place, the boy knows whether his firm is buying or selling certain stocks; he must exercise discrimination in the matter of awarding the orders, should the Board member of the firm happen to be unavailable when the boy receives the order. For example: International Pipe may be selling at 108. A man in Tracy & Middleton's office, who has bought 500 shares of it at 104, wishes to " corral " his profits. He gives an order to the firm to sell the stock, let us say, " at the market," that is, at the ruling market price. Tracy & Middleton immediately telephone over their private line to the Stock Exchange to their Board member to " sell 500 shares of International Pipe at the market." The telephone-boy receives the message and " puts up " Mr. Middleton's number, which means that on the multi-colored, checkered strip on the frieze of the New Street wall, Mr. Middleton's number, 611, appears by means of an electrical device. The moment Mr. Middleton sees that his number is " up," he hastens to the telephone-booth to ascertain what is wanted. Now, if Mr. Middleton delays in answering his number the telephone-boy knows he is absent, and gives the order to a " two-dollar " broker, like Mr. Browning or Mr. Watson, who always hover about the booths looking for orders. He does the same if he knows that Mr. Middleton is very busy executing some other order, or if, in his judgment, the order calls for immediate execution. The two-dollar broker sells the 500 shares of International Pipe to Allen & Smith, and " gives up " Tracy & Middleton on the transaction, that is, he notifies the purchaser that he is acting for T. & M., and Allen & Smith must look to the latter firm — the real sellers — for the stock bought. For this service the broker employed by Tracy & Middleton receives the sum of $2 for each 100 shares, while Tracy & Middleton, of course, charge their customers the regular commission of one eighth of one per cent., or $12.50 per each hundred shares.

Young Hayward attended to his business closely, and when Mr. Middleton was absent from the floor, or busy, he impartially distributed the firm's telephoned buying or selling orders among the two-dollar brokers, for Tracy & Middleton did a

very good commission business indeed.   He was a
nice-looking and nice-acting little chap, was Hayward — clean-faced, polite, and amiable.   The
brokers liked him, and they " remembered " him at
Christmas.   The best memory was possessed by
" Joe " Jacobs, who gave him $25, and insinuated
that he would like to do more of Tracy & Middleton's business than he had been getting.

"But," said Sally, "the firm said I was to
give the order to whichever broker I found first."

" Well," said Jacobs, oleaginously, " I am never
too busy to take orders from such a nice young
fellow as yourself, if you take the trouble to find
me ; and I'll do something nice for you.   Look
here," in a whisper, "if you give me plenty of
business, I'll give you $5 a week."   And he dived
into the mob that was yelling itself hoarse about
the Gotham Gas post.

Hayward's first impulse was to tell his firm
about it, because he felt vaguely that Jacobs would
not have offered him $5 a week if he had not ex-
pected something dishonorable in return.   Before
the market closed, however, he spoke to Willie
Simpson, MacDuff & Wilkinson's boy, whose telephone was next to Tracy & Middleton's.   Sure
enough, Willie expressed great indignation at Jacobs's action.

"It's just like that old skunk," said Willie.
"Five dollars a week, when he can make $100 out
of the firm. Don't you do it, Sally. Why, Jim
Burr, who had the place before you, used to get
$20 a week from old man Grant and $50 a month
from Wolff. You've got a cinch, if you only
know how to work it. Why, they are supposed to
give you fifty cents a hundred." Willie had been
in the business for two years, and he was a very
well-dressed youth, indeed. Sally now understood how he managed it on a salary of $12
a week.

He did not say anything to the firm that day,
nor any other day. And he didn't say anything
to Jacobs in return, but, by Willie's sage advice,
contented himself with merely withholding all orders from that oleaginous personage, until Mr.
Jacobs was moved to remonstrate. And Sally,
who had learned a great deal in a week under
Willie's tuition, answered curtly: "Business is
very bad; the firm is doing hardly anything."

"But Watson told me," said Jacobs, angrily,
"that he was doing a great deal of business for
Tracy & Middleton. I want you to see that I
get my share, or I'll speak to Middleton and find
out what the trouble is."

"Is that so?" said Sally, calmly. "You might

also tell Mr. Middleton that you offered me $5 a week to give you the bulk of our business."

One of the most stringent laws of the Stock Exchange treats of "splitting" commissions. Any member who, in order to increase his business, charges an outsider or another member less than exactly the prescribed amount for buying or selling stocks, is liable to severe penalties. The offer of a two-dollar broker to give a telephone-boy fifty cents for each order of 100 shares secured was obviously a violation of the rule.

Jacobs came down to business at once. "I'll make it $8," he said, conciliatingly.

"Jim Burr, who had the position before me," expostulated Sally, indignantly, "told me he received $25 a week from Mr. Grant, with an extra $10 thrown in from time to time, when Mr. Grant made some lucky turn, to say nothing of what the other men did for him."

Three months before he could not have made this speech had his life depended on it. The rapid development of his character was due exclusively to the "forcing" power of the atmosphere which surrounded him.

"You must be crazy," said Jacobs, angrily. "Why, I never get much more than a thousand shares a week from Tracy & Middleton, and usu-

ally less. Say, you ought to be on the floor. You
are wasting your talent in the telephone business,
you are.   Let's swap places, you and I."

"According to our books," said Sally to the
irate broker, having been duly coached by Mr.
William Simpson, "the last week you did business
for us you did 3,800 shares, and received $76."

"That was an exceptional week. I'll make
it $10," said Jacobs.

"Twenty-five," whispered Sally, determinedly.

"Let's split the difference," murmured Jacobs,
wrathfully.   "I'll give you $15 a week, but you
must see that I get at least 2,500 shares a week."

"All right.   I'll do the best I can for you, Mr.
Jacobs."

And he did, for the other brokers gave him
only twenty-five cents, or at the most fifty cents
per hundred shares.   In the course of a month or
two Sally was in possession of an income of $40 a
week.   And he was only eighteen.

II.

Time ·passed. As it had happened with his
predecessor, so did it happen now with Sally. He
began by speculating, wildly at first, more carefully later on.   He met with sundry reverses, but
he also made some very lucky turns indeed, and

he was "ahead of the game" by a very fair amount
— certainly a sum far greater than any plodding
clerk could save in five years, greater than many
an industrious mechanic saves in his entire life.
From the bucket-shops he went to the Consolidated Exchange. Then he asked Jacobs and the
other two-dollar brokers to let him deal in a small
way with them, which they did out of personal
liking for him, until he had three separate accounts and could "swing a line" of several
hundred shares. He became neither more nor
less than 10,000 other human beings in Wall
Street — moved by the same impulses, actuated
by the same feelings, experiencing the same
emotions, having the same thoughts and the
same views of what they are pleased to call
their "business."

At last the blow fell which Sally had so long
dreaded — he was "promoted" to a clerkship in
Tracy & Middleton's office. The firm meant to
reward him for his devotion to his work, for his
brightness and quickness. From $15 a week they
raised his salary to $25, which they considered
quite generous, especially in view of his youth,
and that he had started three years before with
$8. He was only twenty now. But Sally, know-
ing it meant the abandonment of his lucrative

perquisites as telephone " boy," bemoaned his un-
deserved fate.

He took the money he had made to Mr. Tracy
and told him an interesting story of a rich aunt
and a legacy, and asked him to let him open an
account in the office. Tracy congratulated his
young clerk, took the $6,500, and thereafter Sally
was both an employee and a customer of Tracy &
Middleton.

Addicted to sharp practices though Mr. Tracy
was and loving commissions as he did, he nevertheless sought to curb Sally's youthful propensity
for " plunging," which was as near being kind as
it was possible for a stock-broker to be. But the
money had " come easy." That is why fortunes
won by stock gamblers are lost with apparent
recklessness or stupidity. Sally speculated with
varying success, running up his winnings to $10,-
000, and seeing them dwindle later to $6,000.
But in addition to becoming an inveterate speculator, he gained much valuable experience. And
when he had learned the tricks of the trade he was
taken from the ledgers and turned loose in the
customers' room, to take the latter's orders and
keep them in good humor and tell them the cur-
rent stories, and give them impressively whispered
" tips," and " put them into " various " deals " of

the firm, and see that they traded as often as possible, which meant commissions for the firm.   He became friendly and even familiar with Tracy & Middleton's clients, among whom were some very wealthy men, for a stock-broker's office is a democratic place.   Men who would not have dreamed of taking their Wall Street acquaintances to their homes or to their clubs for a million reasons, all but called each other by their first names there.

He really was a bright, amiable fellow, very obliging — he was paid for it by the firm — and he made the most of his opportunities.   The customers grew to like him exceedingly well, and to think with respect of his judgment, market-wise. One day W. Basil Thornton, one of the wealthiest and boldest customers of the firm, complained of the difficulty of " beating the game " with the heavy handicap of the large brokerage commission.

Jestingly, yet hoping to be taken seriously, Sally said : " Join the New York Stock Exchange or buy me a seat, and form the firm of Thornton & Hayward.   Just think, Colonel, we would have your trade, and you could bring some friends, and I could bring mine, and I think many of these " — pointing to Tracy & Middleton's customers —

"would come over to us. They all think a lot,"
diplomatically, " of your opinions on the market."

Thornton was favorably impressed with the
idea, and Sally saw it. From that moment on he
worked hard to gain the Colonel's confidence. It
was he who gave Thornton the first hint of Tracy
& Middleton's condition, which led to the with-
drawal of Thornton's account — and his own —
from the office. It was a violation of confidence and
of business ethics, but Thornton was very grateful
when, two months later, Tracy & Middleton failed,
under circumstances which were far from credit-
able, and which were discussed at great length by
the Street. He showed his gratitude by adding
a round sum to Sally's $11,500, and Willis N.
Hayward became a member of the New York
Stock Exchange. Shortly afterward the firm of
Thornton & Hayward, Bankers and Brokers, was
formed. Sally, then in his twenty-fifth year, had
become a seasoned Wall Street man.

III.

From the start the new firm did well. Colonel
Thornton and two or three friends who followed
him from Tracy & Middleton's office, all of them
" plungers," were almost enough to keep Hayward
busy on the Exchange executing orders, and,

moreover, new customers were coming in. Had
he been satisfied with this start, and with letting
time do the rest, he would have fared very well.
But he began to speculate for himself, and all
reputable commission men will tell you, with varying degrees of emphasis, that this not only "ties
up" the firm's money, but that no man can
"trade"—speculate—on his own hook and at
the same time do justice to his customers.

Thornton was a rich man, and protected his
own speculations more than amply. He noticed
the development of his young partner's gambling
proclivities, and remonstrated with him—in a
kindly, paternal sort of way.

Sally vowed he would stop.

Within less than three months he had broken
his promise twice, and his unsuccessful operations
in Alabama Coal at one time threatened seriously
to embarrass the firm.

Colonel Thornton came to the rescue.

Sally promised, with a solemnity born of sincere
fear, never to do it again.

But fright lasts but a little space, and memory
is equally short-lived. Wall Street has no room
for men with an excess of timidity or of recollec-
tion. He had gambled before he joined the New
York Stock Exchange. After all, if speculating

were a crime and convictions could be secured in
fifty out of a hundred flagrant instances, one half
the male population of the United States would
perforce consist of penitentiary guards forever en-
gaged in watching over the convicted other half,
Sally told a customer one day.

And then, too, Willis N. Hayward, the Board
member of Thornton & Hayward, was a very different person from Sally, the nice little telephone-
boy of Tracy & Middleton's.   His cheeks were
not pink ; they were mottled.   His eyes were not
clear and ingenuous ; they wer~ shifty and a bit
watery.   He had been in Wall Street eight or
ten years, and he overworked his nerves every day
from 10 A.M. to 3 P.M. on the Stock Exchange ;
also from 5 P.M. to midnight at the café of a big
up-town hotel, where Wall Street men gathered
to talk shop.   His system craved stimulants ;
gambling and liquor were the strongest he knew.

When, after three years, the firm expired by
limitation, Colonel Thornton withdrew.   He had
had enough of Hayward's plunging.   To be sure,
Sally had become a shrewd " trader," and he had
made $75,000 during the big bull boom ; but he
was at heart a " trader," which is to say, a mere
gambler in stocks, and not a desirable commission
man.

But Sally, flushed with success on the bull side, did not worry when Thornton refused to continue the partnership. The slogan was "Buy A. O. T. It's sure to go up!" the initial standing for *Any Old Thing!* The most prosperous period in the industrial and commercial history of the United States begot an epidemic of speculative madness such as was never before known, and probably never again will be. Everybody had money in abundance, and the desire for speculation in superabundance. Sally formed a new firm immediately — Hayward & Co. — with his cashier as partner.

IV.

All mundane things have an end, even bull markets and bear markets. The bull market saw Hayward & Co. doing a good business, as did everybody else in Wall Street. It ended, and the firm's customers, after a few bad "slumps" in prices, were admonished to turn bears in order to recoup their losses. Bears believe prices are too high and should go lower; bulls, optimists, believe the opposite. The public can't sell stocks "short" any more than the average man is left-handed. These customers were no exception, so they did nothing.

Hayward had "overstayed" the bull market, though not disastrously; that is, he was in error regarding the extent and duration of the upward movement of prices. He proceeded to fall into a similar error on the bear, or downward, side. The market had been extremely dull following what the financial writers called a "severe decline," but which meant the loss of millions of dollars by speculators. A panic had been narrowly averted by a timely combination of "powerful interests," after which the market became professional. In the absence of complaisant lambs, the financial cannibals known as "room traders" and "pikers" tried to "scalp eighths" out of each other for weeks — to take advantage of fractional fluctuations instead of waiting for big movements. Hayward's customers, like everybody else's customers, were not speculating. So he used their money to protect his own speculations. Office expenses were numerous and heavy, and commissions few and light.

Hayward was very bearish. He had sold stocks, sharing the belief of the majority of his fellows, that the lowest prices had not been reached. As a result he was heavily "short," and he could not "cover" at a profit, because prices had advanced very slowly, but very steadily.

One day a big gambler in Chicago, bolder or keener than his Eastern brethren, thought the time was ripe for a "bull" or upward movement in general, and particularly in Consolidated Steel Rod Company's stock. He was the chairman of the board of directors. Mr. William G. Dorr decided upon a plan whereby the stock would be made attractive to that class of speculative investors, so to speak, who liked to buy stocks making generous disbursements of profits to their holders. Mr. Dorr's plan was kept a secret. The first step consisted of sending in large buying orders, handled by prominent brokers, and synchronously the publication, in the daily press, of various items, all reciting the wonderful prosperity of the Consolidated Steel Rod Company and its phenomenal earnings; also the unutterable cheapness of the stock at the prevailing price. Mr. Dorr and associates, of course, had previously taken advantage of the big "slump" or fall in values to buy back at 35 the same stock they had sold to the public some weeks before at 70. Having acquired this cheap stock, they "manipulated" — by means of further purchase — the price so that they could sell out at a profit.

It so happened, however, that once before dividend rumors about "Con. Steel Rod" had been disseminated, with the connivance of Dorr, and they had not come true, to the great detriment of credulous buyers and the greater profit of the insiders, who were "short" of the stock "up to their necks" — a typical bit of stock-jobbing whereat other and more artistic stock-jobbers had expressed the greatest indignation. Instead of putting the stock on a dividend-paying basis, the directors had decided — at the last hour — that it would not be conservative to do so, whereupon the stock had "broken" seventeen points. The lambs lost hundreds of thousands of dollars; the insiders gained as much. It was a "nice turn."

Hayward remembered this, and when the stock, after several days of conspicuous activity and steady advances, rose to 52, he promptly sold "short" 5,000 shares — believing that the barefaced manipulation would not raise the stock much above that figure, and that before long it must decline. Only a month previously it had sold at 35 and nobody wanted any of it. He was all the more decided in his opinion that the "top" had been reached by prices, because Mr. Dorr, in a Chicago paper, had stated that the stockholders would probably receive an entire year's dividend at one fell swoop by reason of the unexampled prosperity in the steel rod trade. Such an action was unprecedented. It had been talked about at various times in connection with other stocks, but it had never come true. Why should it come true in this instance?

Hayward, familiar with Dorr's record, promptly "coppered" his "tip" to buy, banking on Dorr's consistent mendacity. But Mr. William G. Dorr, shrewdest and boldest of all Western stock gamblers, fooled everybody — he actually told the truth. That week the directors did exactly as he had predicted. When a speculator of his calibre lies he fools only one half — the foolish half — of the Street. When he tells the truth he deceives everybody. Before Wall Street could recover from the shock the price of the stock was up 5 points, which meant that Hayward was out $25,000 on that deal alone. But, in addition, the general list was carried upward sympathetically. The semi-paralyzed bulls regained confidence as they saw the successful outcome of the Chicago gambler's manœuvres in Consolidated Steel Rod. Money rates and bear hopes fell; stock values and bull courage rose! Hayward began "covering" Steel Rod. He "bought in" 5,000 shares, and after he finished he had lost $26,750 by the deal. He was still "short" about 12,000 shares of other stocks, on which his

"paper" losses, at the last quoted prices, were over
$35,000; but if he tried to buy back such a large
amount of stock in a market so sensitive to any
kind of bull impetus, he would send prices upward
in a jiffy, increasing his own losses very materially.

He went to his office that morning in a tremor.
He consulted the cashier, and found he had only
$52,000 at the bank, of which two thirds be-
longed to his customers. He was already, morally
speaking, an embezzler. He was ruined if he
didn't cover, and he was ruined if he did. His
"seat" on the Stock Exchange was worth possibly
$40,000, not a cent more; and as he personally
owed his out-of-town correspondents nearly $38,-
000, he could not avoid being hopelessly ruined.
Moreover, his bankruptcy would not be an
"honest" failure, for, as he told himself bitterly,
after the harm was done, "I had no business to
speculate on my own hook with other people's
money."

He had felt it rather than had seen it coming,
for, gambler-like, he had closed his eyes and had
buried his head in the sand of hope, trusting in
luck to protect him from punishment. But now
he was face to face with the question that every
gambler dreads: "If I stood to lose all, how
desperate a risk would I take in order to get it

back?" The answer is usually so appallingly thief-like that the numerous Haywards of the Stock Exchange and the Board of Trade forthwith stop thinking with a suddenness that does credit to the remnants of their honesty. But it haunts them, does the ominous question and the commenced but unfinished answer.

As he left his office to go to the "Board Room" he put to himself the fateful query. But he would not let himself answer it until he had stopped at "Fred's," the official barroom of the Stock Exchange, and had taken a stiff drink of raw whiskey. Then the answer came.

He was ruined anyhow. If he failed without further ado, that is, without increasing his liabilities, he would be cursed by twenty-five of his customers and by fifteen of his fellow-brokers who were "lending" stocks to him. But if he made one last desperate effort, he might pull out of the hole; or, at the worst, why, the number of cursing customers would remain the same, but the fellow-brokers would rise to twenty or thirty.

He took another stiff drink. The market had become undoubtedly a bull market. The bears had been fighting the advance, and there still remained a stubborn short interest in certain stocks, as, for example, in American Sugar Company stock. Now if that short interest could be stampeded it might mean an eight or ten-point advance. If he bought 10,000 or 15,000 shares and sold them at an average profit of four or five points, he would put off the disaster, and if he made ten points he would be a great operator. He had, to be sure, no business to buy even 1,000 shares of Sugar; but then he had no business to be on the verge of bankruptcy.

The liquor was potent. Sally said to himself, aggrievedly: "I might as well be hung for a flock as for one measly old mutton."

He walked a trifle unsteadily from "Fred's" across the narrow asphalted New Street to the Stock Exchange. He paused at the entrance. There was no escape. Unless he could make a lucky strike, he would fail ignominiously.

"Pike's Peak or bust!" he muttered to himself, and walked into the big room.

"Good-morning, Mr. Hayward," said the doorkeeper. Hayward nodded absently, caught himself repeating, "Pike's Peak or bust!" and walked straight toward the Sugar post.

He began to bid for stock. One thousand shares at 116; he got it. Another thousand; it was forthcoming at $116\frac{1}{8}$. A third thousand; somebody was glad to sell it at $116\frac{1}{2}$. So far, so bad. Then he bid 117 for 2,500 shares, and it was promptly sold. But when he bid "117 for any part of 5,000!" the crowd hesitated; the brokers were not altogether sure Hayward was "good for it"; his ability to pay for the stock was not undoubted. So Sally, taking advantage of the hesitation, bid $117\frac{1}{4}$ and $117\frac{1}{2}$ for 5,000 Sugar, at which price "Billy" Thatcher, a two-dollar broker, sold it to him. It made 10,500 shares Hayward had bought, and the stock had risen only $1\frac{1}{2}$ points. The shorts were not frightened a wee bit. But Sally was. He rushed out of the crowd to his telephone and made a pretence of "reporting" the transactions to his office, as he would have done had they been *bona fide* purchases. He was followed by a hundred sharply curious — and curiously sharp — eyes. They saw him hold the telephone receiver to his ear with an expression of great interest, as if he were listening to an important message. But the only message he heard was that of his heart-beats, that seemed to say, almost articulately: "You have played and you have lost; you have played and you have lost. Therefore, you are that much worse off than before. You must play again — *and not lose!*"

He left his telephone and rushed back to the Sugar crowd. He was less excited, less like a

drunken man; his face was no longer flushed, but
pale. And anon there flashed upon him, as if in
candent letters, the words *Pike's Peak or bust!*
But *Pike's Peak* glowed dully, feebly, while the
alternative was of a lurid splendor. And he
blinked his eyes and made a curious impatient
motion with his hand, as one waves away an an-
noying insect.

He gave an order for 5,000 Sugar to his friend,
Newton Hartley.

"Is this for yourself, Sally?" asked Hartley.

"No. It's for one of the biggest men in the
Street, Newt. It's all right. Absolutely O. K."

And thus reassured, Hartley bought the stock.
The price was 118. The seller would hold Hartley responsible for the purchase money if Hayward " laid down " — refused to pay.

Sally wiped his forehead twice, quite unneces-
sarily. The shorts were not stampeding. Any
attempt to sell out the 15,000 shares he had
bought would result only in depressing the price,
five points at least. It was worse than bad, the
outlook for him.

He gave another order to buy 5,000 shares to
" Billy " Lansing, an old and reliable two-dollar
broker, but Lansing declined it. He tried another, but the order was not accepted. They mis-

trusted him; but he could not even bluster, for they excused themselves on the ground of having important orders elsewhere. So he had recourse to another personal friend — J. G. Thompson.

"Joe, buy 5,000 Sugar."

"Are you sober?" said Thompson, seriously.

"See for yourself," answered Sally, laughingly. He had nerve. "Old man, I've got a very big order from one of the biggest men in the Street. Some important developments are going on."

"Sally, are you sure you've got an order from some one else?" asked the unconvinced broker. His incredulity was obviously in the nature of an insult, but it was pardonable, for there was too much at stake.

"Joe, come over to the office and I'll show you — Really, I can't tell you. But I can advise you, as a friend, to buy Sugar for all you are worth." And as he uttered the lie he looked straight into Thompson's eyes.

"Hayward, are you sure? Are you sure you're not making a mistake?" He wanted the commission of $100, but he did not feel certain of his friend.

"Oh, hell, no. I've got a lot more to buy. It's all right. Go ahead, Joe."

And Joe went ahead. He bought the 5,000

shares. The stock rose to 119½, and Hayward,
warned by his experience with Hartley and Thompson, did not ask either friend or foe to buy another
5,000 shares for him. What he did was to dis-
tribute buying orders for 10,000 shares in lots of
500. Brokers now accepted his orders, for they
were not so large as to be dangerous. And the
stock rose to 122¾. A few shorts were frightened.
He might win out after all ; he might make Pike's
Peak. He began to bid up the stock. He even
bought " cash " stock, that is, stock for which he
paid cash, had to pay cash outright, receiving the
certificates forthwith, presumably to hand over to
some investor of millions. Everybody on the
" floor " was talking about Hayward. The entire
market had risen in sympathy with Sugar.

But at 124 it seemed as if the entire capital
stock was for sale. He ceased buying. He had
accumulated 38,000 shares. To pay for the
stock necessitated about six and one-half millions! But if he could unload on an average
of only 122 he might " come out even " in his
other troubles.

He gave an order to sell 10,000 shares to a
broker to whom he had always been a good friend.
It was a fatal mistake. The broker, Louis W.
Wechsler, had previously sold 1,000 shares to

Hayward for " cash " at 122.   He suspected what was coming, and declining the order, he himself went to Hayward's office and asked for a check. The cashier sought to put him off with excuses, and Wechsler now being certain of the true state of affairs, returned to the Board and began to sell Sugar short for his own account.   If a crash came he would make instead of losing it.   Hayward was sure to be ruined, and Wechsler told himself sophistically that he was only profiting by the inevitable.   In the meantime Sally had sold the 10,000 shares through another broker, and the price had declined to 121¾.   But Wechsler's 5,000 shares put it down to 120½.   And somebody else sold more, and the shorts recovered from their fright, and the fatal hour was approaching when Hayward would have to settle.   Pike's Peak or bust !   He did, indeed, need a veritable Pike's Peak of dollars to pay for the 28,000 Sugar he had on hand.   So he busted.

He threw up his hands.   He acknowledged defeat to himself.   The tension was over.   He was no longer excited, but cool, almost cynical.   On one of the little slips of paper on which brokers jot down memoranda of their transactions he scribbled a message in lead pencil.   It was his last official lie, and would cost Hartley and Thompson and other friends, as well as his customers, many thousands of dollars. It was as follows :

"Owing to the refusal of their bank to extend the usual facilities to them, Hayward & Co. are compelled to announce their suspension."

"Boy!" he yelled. And he gave the bit of paper to one of the Exchange messenger boys in gray. "Take this to the Chairman."

And he walked slowly, almost swaggeringly, out of the New York Stock Exchange — for the last time — as the Chairman pounded with his gavel until the usual crowd gathered about the rostrum, and listened to the announcement of the failure of "Sally" Hayward, who began as a nice little telephone-boy and ended as a stock-gambler.

A THEOLOGICAL TIPSTER

A THEOLOGICAL TIPSTER

At first Wall Street thought that Silas Shaw's "religiousness" was an affectation. What purpose the Old Man desired to serve by the calculated notoriety of his church affiliations no one could tell. It is true that many ingenious theories were advanced, some going so far as to hint at repentance. But deep in the hearts of his fellow-brokers, and of his friends and his victims alike, was the belief that old Shaw, in some not generally known way, made practical use of his ostentatious enthusiasm for things churchly as politicians resort to more or less obvious devices to "capture the German vote" or to "please the Irish element."

One day, after a series of skirmishes and a final pitched battle in "South Shore" between the Old Man and the bears, when the pelts of the latter, after the capitulation, added nearly a half million to the old fellow's bank account, certain luminaries of the Methodist Episcopal Church were called into consultation. Silas Shaw had long thought about it; and now there was much conferring and more or less arid and misplaced sermonizing by the the-

ologians and much soothing talk by the Old Man's
lawyers ; and more Methodist clergymen and more
lawyers and more talk ; and then a real estate
agent and an architect and a leading banker and,
at last, just one check from the Old Man.

The next day the newspapers announced that
the Shaw Theological Seminary had been founded
and endowed by Mr. Silas Shaw. But even after
the Old Man had devoted his ursine spoils to this
praiseworthy object, Wall Street continued skep-
tical.

And, yet, Wall Street made a mistake — as it
often does in its judgment of its leaders. Silas
Shaw really had a soft spot in his tape-wound and
ticker-dented old heart for all things ecclesiastical.
Next to being a power in the Street he loved to
be regarded as one of the pillars of his church.
He heard with pleasure, of week days, the wakeful
staccato sound of the ticker ; but on Sundays he
certainly enjoyed the soothing cadences of familiar
hymns. And if more than one hardened broker
expressed picturesque but unreproducible opinions
of the old man, so also more than one enthusiastic
young minister could tell pleasant stories of how
the old stock gambler received him and responded
to the fervent appeal for the funds wherewith
many a little backwoods church was built.

Shaw's generosity was so notorious among the church people that the Reverend Doctor Ramsdell, pastor of the Steenth Street Methodist Episcopal Church and a trustee of the Shaw Theological Seminary, felt no embarrassment in applying to him for assistance. It was not Shaw's church, but in Dr. Ramsdell's charge there were one or two bankers well known in Wall Street and several members of the New York Stock Exchange. It seemed particularly fitting to the Rev. Dr. Ramsdell that the name of Silas Shaw, followed by a few figures, should head a subscription list. It was desired to erect a Protestant Chapel in Oruro, Bolivia — the most uncivilized of all the South American "republics."

"Good-morning, Brother Shaw; I trust you are well."

"Tolerable, tolerable, thank'ee kindly," replied the sturdy old gambler. "What brings you down to this sinful section? Doing some missionary work, eh? I wish you'd begin among those da — er — dandy young bears."

"Ah, yes," said the Rev. Dr. Ramsdell, eagerly. "It is precisely à *propos* of missionary work." And he told Silas Shaw all about the plan for carrying the light into Bolivia by building the only Protestant chapel in Oruro, where it was incredibly tenebrous — worse than darkest Africa. The reverend doctor hoped, nay, he knew, in view of Brother Shaw's well-known devotion to the glorious work of redeeming their benighted Bolivian brethren, that he could count upon him, etc. ; and the subscription list ——

"My dear Dr. Ramsdell," interrupted Shaw, "I never sign subscription lists. When I give, I give ; and I don't want everybody to know how much I've given."

"Well, Brother Shaw, you need not sign your name. I'll put you down as X. Y. Z.," he smiled encouragingly.

"No, no ; don't put me down at all."

The good doctor looked so surprised and so woebegone that Shaw laughed.

"Cheer up, Doctor. I tell you what I'll do ; I'll buy some Erie for you. Yes, sirree ; that's the best thing I can do. What do you say to that?" And he looked at the doctor, triumphantly.

"Ahem ! — I am not — are you sure it will prove a — ahem ! — a desirable investment? You see, I do not — ah — know much about Wall Street."

"Neither do I. And the older I grow the less I know."

The reverend doctor ventured a tentative smile of semi-incredulity.

"That's right, Doctor.   But we'll make something for you.   The blooming, I mean, benighted Bohemians——"

"Ahem! — Bolivians, Brother Shaw."

"I meant Bolivians.   They must have a chance for their souls.   John," to a clerk; "buy 500 shares of Erie at the market."

"Yes, sir," said John, disappearing into the telephone booth.   To buy, "at the market" meant to buy at the prevailing or market price.

"Brother Shaw, I am extremely grateful to you. This matter is very close to my heart, I assure you.   And — ah — will — when will I know if the — ah — investment turns out profitably?"

"Oh, have no fears on that score.   We shall make the stock market contribute to your missionary fund.   All you'll have to do is to look on the financial page of your paper every evening and keep posted."

"I fear, Brother Shaw," said Dr. Ramsdell, deprecatingly, "that I shall have no little trouble in — ah — keeping posted."

"Not at all.   See, here," and he took up his paper and turned to the stock tables.   "Draw up your chair, Doctor.   You see, here is Erie.   Yesterday, on transactions of 18,230 shares, Erie Railroad stock sold as high as 64¾ and as low as 63¼, the last or closing sale being at 64½. The numbers mean dollars per share. It was very strong. Haven't you got a report on that 500 Erie yet, John?"

"Yes, sir," said John. "Sixty-five and one-eighth."

"You see, Doctor, the stock is still going up. Well, every day when you look on the table you will see at what price Erie stock is selling. If it is more than 65⅛, why, that will show you are making money. Every point up, that is, every unit, will mean that your missionary fund is $500 richer."

"And — Brother Shaw — ahem! — if it should be — ah — less?"

"What's the use of thinking such things, Dr. Ramsdell? All you have to remember is that I am going to make some money for you; and that I paid 65⅛ for the stock I bought."

"You really think ———"

"Have no fears, Doctor. You understand, of course, that it is well not to give such matters undue publicity."

"Of course, of course," assented the doctor. "I understand." But he did not.

"Nothing more, Doctor?"

"No; I thank you very much, Brother Shaw. I — er — most sincerely hope my — ah — your — I should say — ah — our investment, may result in — ah — favorably for our Bolivian Missionary Fund.   Thanks very much."

"Don't mention it, Doctor.   And don't you worry.   We will come out O.K.   You'll hear from me in a week or two.   Good-morning."

The reverend doctor went across the street to the office of one of his parishioners, Walter H. Cranston, a stock broker.

Mr. Cranston was bemoaning the appalling lack of business and making up his mind about certain Delphic advice he contemplated giving his timid customers, in order to make them "trade," which would mean commissions, when Dr. Ramsdell's card was brought.

"Confound him, what does he want to come around, bothering a man at his business for?" he thought.   But he said: "Show him in, William."

"Good-morning, Brother Cranston."

"Why, good-morning, Dr. Ramsdell.   To what do I owe this unexpected pleasure?"

"I've called to see you about our Missionary Fund.   You know I take a great deal of interest in it.   We desire to build a chapel in Bolivia, where the light is needed, Brother Cranston, as much as in China, I assure you. And it is so much nearer home."

" Doctor, I really — " began Cranston, with an injured air.

" I want your valuable autograph to head the subscription list," said the clergyman with an air he endeavored to make arch and playful. " Don't refuse me."

" Why don't you try some well-known person ? " said Cranston, modestly.

" To tell you the truth, Brother Cranston, I did try Silas Shaw." And he added, hastily, " Not but that you are sufficiently well-known for my purpose."

" What did the old ras — the Old Man say ? "

" He said he never signed subscription lists."

" Didn't he give you anything at all ? "

" Oh, yes ; he — er — he did something for me." The doctor's face assumed a portentous air.

Cranston's eyes brightened. " What was that?" he said.

" Well," said the clergyman, hesitatingly, " he said we would come out O. K. Those are his own words, Brother Cranston."

" Yes ? " Cranston's face did not look promising for Bolivian enlightenment.

"Yes. He—er—told me he would make the stock market contribute to the fund."

"Indeed!" Cranston showed a lively interest.

"Yes. I suppose since you are in the same business, there is no harm in telling you that he bought some stock for me. Five hundred shares, it was. Do you think, Brother Cranston, that—er—that will mean much? You see, I have the fund very close to my heart; that is why I ask."

"It depends," said Cranston, very carelessly, "upon what stock he bought for you."

"It was Erie Railroad stock."

"Of course, Dr. Ramsdell, your profits will depend upon the price you paid." This also in a tone of utter indifference.

"It was Brother Shaw who paid. The price was $65\frac{1}{8}$."

"Aha!" said Cranston. "So the Old Man is bullish on Erie, is he?"

"I do not know what you mean, but I know he told me I should read the paper every day and see how much above $65\frac{1}{8}$ the price went; and that I would surely hear from him."

"I sincerely hope you will, Doctor. Let me see, will $100 do? Very well, I'll make out a check for you. Here it is. And now, Doctor, will you excuse me? We are very busy, indeed.

Good-morning, Dr. Ramsdell. Call again any time you happen to be down this way." And he almost pushed the good man out of the office in his eagerness to be rid of him.

No sooner had the ground-glass door closed on the Rev. Dr. Ramsdell than Cranston rushed to the telephone and put in an order to buy 1,000 shares of Erie at the best possible price. By doing this before he notified his friends he proved that he himself firmly believed in Erie ; also, he bought his stock ahead of theirs and thereby, in all likelihood, bought it cheaper. He then rushed into the customers' room and yelled : " Hi, there ! Everybody get aboard Erie ! Silas Shaw is bullish as Old Nick on it. I get this absolutely straight. I've thought all along the old rascal was quietly picking it up. It's his movement and no mistake. There ought to be ten points in it if you buy now."

The firm of Cranston & Melville bought in all, that day, for themselves and their customers, 6,200 shares of Erie, doing as much as anyone else to advance the price to 66½.

All that week the reverend doctor was busy collecting subscriptions for the Bolivian Missionary Fund. He was a good soul and an enthusiast on the subject of that particular subscription list.

So, he told his parishioners how Brother Cranston had given $100 and Brother Baker, another Wall Street man, $250, and Brother Shaw had promised — he told this with an amused smile, as if at the incongruity of it — to make the stock market contribute to the fund ! Brother Shaw had done this by buying some stock for him and had assured him, in his picturesque way, that it would come out O. K. in a week or two. Everybody to whom he told that fact developed curiosity regarding the name of the stock itself. They showed it in divers ways, according to their various temperaments. And as he had told some he felt that he should not discriminate against others ; so, he told to all, impartially, the name of the stock. It would not harm Brother Shaw, he supposed — and he supposed rightly. He experienced, in a gentle, benevolent, half-unconscious sort of way, something akin to the great Wall Street delight — that of " giving a straight tip " to appreciative friends. The Bolivian Missionary Fund grew even beyond the good man's optimistic expectations.

But a strange, a very strange thing happened : Erie stock, according to the doctor's daily perusal of the dry financial pages, had been fluctuating between 65 and 67. On the following Tuesday,

to his intense surprise, the stock table recorded:
"Highest, $65\frac{3}{4}$; lowest, 62; last, $62\frac{5}{8}$." On
Wednesday the table read: "Highest, $62\frac{1}{2}$; lowest, 58; last 58." On Thursday, there was a ray
of hope —— the stock sold as high as 60 and closed
at $59\frac{1}{2}$. But on Friday there was a bad break
and Erie touched $54\frac{1}{8}$, just $11\frac{1}{8}$ points below what
the Bolivian Missionary Fund's stock had cost.
And, on Saturday, the stock declined to 50, closing at $51\frac{1}{4}$.

That Sunday the Reverend Doctor Henry W.
Ramsdell preached to the gloomiest congregation
in Gotham. Wherever he turned his gaze he met
reproachful looks —— accusing eyes, full of bitterness
or of anger or of sadness. An exception was Mr.
Silas Shaw, who had come, as he often did, to hear
his friend, Dr. Ramsdell, preach. His eyes beamed
benignantly on the pastor throughout the long
sermon. He looked as if he felt, Dr. Ramsdell
thought, inexplicably contented. Had he forgotten his promise —— the promise from which benighted Bolivia expected so much?

The two men met after the service. Dr. Ramsdell's manner was constrained; Mr. Shaw's affable.

"Good-morning, Doctor," said the grizzled old
operator. "I've carried a small piece of paper in

my pocket for some days, in the hope of meeting you. Here it is." And he handed a check for $5,000 to the clergyman.

"Why — er — I — er — I — didn't — the stock — er — go down ? "

"Sure ! "

"How is it then that ———"

"Oh, that's all right. It came out just as I expected. That's why you get the check."

"But — ahem ! — didn't you buy 500 shares for me ? "

"Yes ; but after you left I sold 10,000 shares between 65 and 67. Your congregation, Doctor, developed a remarkable bullishness on Erie." He chuckled gleefully. "It was to them that I sold the stock ! "

"But my — ahem ! — impression was that you said the stock would go up."

"Oh, no. I never said that. I merely told you we'd come out O. K. And I guess we have." He laughed joyously. "It's all right, Doctor ; those pesky Bolivians will be enlightened, you bet."

"But," said the doctor, with a very red face, fingering the check, hesitatingly, "I don't know whether to accept it or not."

"Oh, you're not robbing me," the old stock

gambler assured him, gaily. "I made out quite well; quite well, thank you."

"I —— I —— mean ——" stammered the clergyman, "I don't know whether it is right to ——"

Shaw frowned. "Put that check in your pocket," he said, sharply. "You earned it."

THE END

9 781163 940921